Treasures of a
Grandmother's Heart

Treasures of a Grandmother's Heart

Finding Pearls of Wisdom in Everyday Moments

by Esther Burroughs

New Hope Publishers

Birmingham, Alabama

New Hope Publishers
P. O. Box 12065
Birmingham, AL 35202-2065
www.newhopepubl.com

Library of Congress Cataloging-in-Publication Data
Burroughs, Esther.
Treasures of a grandmother's heart : finding pearls of wisdom in every
    day moments / by Esther Burroughs.
    p. cm.
ISBN 1-56309-722-2 (hardcover)
    1. Grandmothers--Religious life. I. Title.
BV4528.5 .B87   2002
242'.6431--dc21
        2001007412

Cover and page design by Diana Lawrence

ISBN: 1-56309-722-2

N024121 • 0602 • 5M2

Dedication

To my grandchildren

~

How the world will glow with beauty
When love shines in
And the heart rejoice in duty
When love shines in.
Trials will be sanctified
And the soul in peace abide
Life will all be glorified
When love shines in.

—from a note my grandmother Esther
wrote to my mother, September 10, 1934

Contents

Introduction

When that first grandchild is born, a "grandmother" is also born.

A telephone call changed my life...literally! Our daughter, Melody, had called to announce that she and Will were expecting their first child. Bob and I could hardly contain our excitement and joy. I had many fond memories of my own grandparents from my years of growing up. Now I looked with excitement toward this new journey of becoming a grandparent.

I found myself listening more carefully to other grandparent stories. I had really important questions in my heart:

> *What will this grandchild call me?*
> *Will this grandchild like me?*
> *How can I be a good grandparent?*
> *What does it mean...to be a grandparent?*

A friend once said, "Being a grandparent is belonging to a select club. The only way you can get into the club is if your children cooperate. When this happens, you'll be a lifetime member—with no fees, but many expenses!"

No one needs to take a course in "Grandparenting 101"...when the time comes, you'll know what to do. Your name may be Grandma, Grans, Mimi, Nana, Gogo, Mammaw, Gamma, or a host of other special names. But whatever the name, it denotes a very special position in life...both for you and for your grandchild.

"Bop," the name our grandchildren have given my husband, found these wonderful words about a grandmother, written by an anonymous eight-year old girl, and set them to music:

~

What a Grandmother Is

A grandmother is a lady who has no
little children of her own,
so she likes other people's little folks.

A grandfather is a "man grandmother."
He goes for walks with boys,
and they talk about fishin' and things like that.

Grandmas don't have to do anything
except to be there.

They are older, so they shouldn't play hard or run.

It is enough if they take us to the market
where the pretend horse is,
and have plenty of dimes ready.

And if they take us for walks, they slow down
at things like pretty leaves or caterpillars.

They never say, "Hurry up!"

Usually grandmas are fat.
But not too fat to tie a kid's shoe.

They wear glasses, and they can take out
their teeth *and* their gums!

They don't have to be smart...
only to answer questions like,
"Why dogs chase cats?"
or "How come God isn't married?"

When they read to us, they don't skip words,
or mind if it is the same story over again.

Everyone should have one,
for grandmas are the only grown-ups
who've got time.

And this is what my grandma means to me.

~

As a grandparent you begin to understand unconditional love—maybe for the first time. In fact, one of the virtues people often attribute to their grandmothers is unconditional love. At times, it feels very much like God's love. I have learned unconditional love from my grandkids, too—maybe even more than they have learned it from me.

In the summer of 2001, Bob and I went to Pell City, Alabama, to visit my 95-year-old father. In the course of our two-day visit, we found ourselves making the quick 45-minute drive to the Birmingham airport. Our son's family would be flying out of there, and we thought we might just get a hug from those grandtwins!

We called and made arrangements to meet them at a nearby Chick-fil-A.

I can't tell you the excitement we felt: A visit with our grandkids—even if for only 30 minutes! As we drove into the parking lot, I saw them sitting inside. We literally ran from our car. The moment we opened the door, the twins jumped out of their chairs and ran into our arms, calling as they ran, "Nana! Bop! Nana! Bop!" Walker, our grandson, ran to me as Milligan, our granddaughter, ran to Bop.

We scooped them up, hugged them, and sat down together. Walker, hugging close to my side as he ate his chicken nuggets, looked up with those big, brown eyes and said, "Nana, I go your house?" How is it that my little red-headed grandson's smile and words can reduce me to a puddle of joy? I squeezed him even closer.

God created mothers with special nurturing spirits. This means that grandmothers have a double portion...as both a mother and as a grandmother.

An excellent model for godly grandparenting can be found in 2 Timothy 3:14-15:

"But you must continue in the things which you have learned and been assured of, knowing from whom you have learned them and that from childhood you have known the Holy Scriptures, which are able to make you wise for salvation through faith which is in Christ Jesus."

God gifts us as grandparents both to play and to pray.

From his childhood, Timothy was taught not only by his mother, but also by his grandmother. I can picture those two women praying for young Timothy on their knees and teaching him God's Word; just as my daughter and I pray together over the phone for her girls—my grandgirls.

What a Godly heritage Timothy received! His father is not mentioned—perhaps he died during his early years. Paul assures young Timothy that he prays for him daily through his tears. He remembers Timothy's faith: *"which first lived in your grandmother Lois and in your mother Eunice, and I am persuaded, now lives in you also"* (2 Timothy 1:5 NIV).

Paul pours out his heart for his son-in-the-ministry, urging Timothy to *"guard the good deposit that was entrusted to you"* (2 Timothy 1:14 NIV). And this, dear reader, is what you and I are called to do as grandmothers: We are to pass on to the next generation our faith stories; telling them over and over. We must take seriously our task as grandparents.

Travel with me now through this collection of stories, ideas, thoughts, and prayers as we continue in our journey of grandparenting....

"Nana, Just Stay Long Enough"

For many years, my daughter and her family lived in Atlanta, Georgia. In my travels to and from my speaking engagements, it sometimes worked out for me to spend a night or two with them. Whenever I was there, I would always ask for the privilege of reading the bedtime stories to my grandgirls ...and my grandgirls begged for me to do it. They knew that I would read as many stories as they liked...*and that I did not skip pages!* I knew better, for in the past I had done just that...skipped a page or two.

Mothers are usually in a hurry. Grandmothers are not. That is why, as grandmothers, we must choose to be involved with our grandkids. They need the balance of mothers and grandmothers. Children can sense when we are in a hurry. Grandmothers can help slow the pace for our grandkids.

On one such occasion, I read my oldest grandchild, Anna Esther, all her favorite stories, said prayers with her, and then kissed her good night. As I stood to leave the room, she looked up and said, "Nana, could you just stay long enough for me to tell you how much I love you?"

My heart stood still. I turned back and bent down to hold her again, the only way to respond to such precious words. She reached up, took my face in her hands, and pulled me ever so close, whispering, "Nana, I could never get done telling you how much I love you."

My tears flowed as I left the room. I wanted to find a quiet place to cherish Anna Esther's words and allow them to settle in my heart. I then wrote those precious words in my journal so I would never forget them.

This is not just a "grandmother story." It's a God story! When God sent His Son, Jesus, to die on a cross, His outstretched arms reached out to all humanity with this message:

 "I could never get done telling you how much I love you."

Jesus took the burden of our sin, nailed it to a cross, and signed it with his own blood, sealing His love story forever. He never stops loving us—no matter what we have done, where we have been, or what we will do. He proclaimed his message: "It is finished!"

Like a grandchild who declares, "I could never get done telling you how much I love you," our heavenly Father says to us, "I will never get over my love for you." Cherish His words, and read 1st Thessalonians 3:12 again and again: *"May the Master pour on the love so it fills your lives and splashes on everyone around you."* (THE MESSAGE)

♥ treasures of the heart

♥ Copy 1 Thessalonians 3:12 onto this journal page. Then write your own paraphrase of this verse. Make it personal.

_____

_____

_____

_____

_____

_____

_____

_____

_____

_____

_____

_____

_____

_____

_____

_____

_____

_____

_____

pearls of wisdom

Write a "love letter" to one of your grandkids today. Splash your love on him or her by sharing the qualities you most admire in him or her. Close your letter with a Scripture verse.

Copy your love letter in this journal, so when your grandchild visits you can share the letter with him or her and share the blessing together.

_____

_____

_____

_____

_____

_____

_____

_____

_____

_____

_____

_____

_____

_____

A Happy Ending!

Mrs. Arvella Schuller is the wife of Dr. Robert Schuller, pastor at the Crystal Cathedral in Anaheim, California. She shares one of her own "grandmother" stories in the book, *Friends for Life*, by Jim and Sheila Coleman.

One night, Arvella agreed to babysit her daughter Sheila's four rambunctious boys, ages one through four. As Sheila and her husband, Jim, rushed to get out the door on time, they hurried through last-minute instructions about diapers, bottles, and emergency phone numbers. "Oh, yes," Sheila added, "Here's the medicine for Nicky's bronchitis. Give him a teaspoonful before he goes to bed."

It was a hectic evening, but Arvella didn't forget the medicine! Nicky make a terrible face and fussed a lot, but she forced the medicine into his mouth. When he tried to spit it out, she held his lips shut until he swallowed. Figuring it wouldn't hurt to check the bottle just to be certain the dosage was correct, Arvella made a horrible discovery! She had given baby Nicky the dog's medicine!

Horrified, she called the poison control center, only to be put on hold. When someone finally came back to the phone, he suggested Arvella call a vet!

The story does have a happy ending. The medicine was only a combination of vitamins. There was nothing harmful in the concoction at all. In fact, when Arvella called her daughter the next morning to check on Nicky, Sheila responded cheerily: "Well, I checked him over this morning. His hair is pretty shiny, his nose is wet, and he's been barking orders at me ever since he got up."

⁓

I hope you're laughing! Go ahead...laugh long and loud! Smile! Smile broadly! We all need more laughter and joy these days!

⁓

Grandmothers don't get it right all the time. But laughter is a simple and helpful prescription for life's ills and struggles. The great news is that researchers have now discovered that laughter releases the same endorphins as exercise. So put away your walking gear and get on your laughing gear! It makes most situations better, and it helps the medicine of life go down. A wise king once said, "*A cheerful heart is good medicine, but a crushed spirit dries up the bones*" (Proverbs 17:22 NIV).

As grandmothers, let us choose laughter on this journey. We will refresh ourselves as well as our grandchildren.

♥ treasures of the heart

♥ Write down one or more of the funniest events of your life. You must have many. This will leave happy memories for your children and grandchildren to discover and read after you are gone.

_____

_____

_____

_____

_____

_____

_____

_____

_____

_____

_____

_____

_____

_____

_____

_____

_____

_____

♥ treasures of the heart

♥ In the Scriptures, research the word "joy." Enter your favorite "joy" verses in your journal. Write down reflections on why these verses are precious to you.

_____

_____

_____

_____

_____

_____

_____

_____

_____

_____

● pearls of wisdom

● Purchase a book of clean, kid-friendly jokes from a local bookstore, and email your grandchildren a joke a week.

● Anytime your grandchildren are with you, make room for laughter!

An Answer to Prayer

I had prayed for her since August 5,1989—since the time I knew she was to be born. I did not know at that time, of course, that the new baby would be a girl—or that my daughter, Melody, would give her the name Anna Esther Reid, to honor her great grandmother and her grandmother. My prayer journals recall that name many times over the past 12 years. Praying mothers and grandmothers become sensitive to the working of the Holy Spirit in the lives of their children.

My daughter and I knew in the early months of 2001 that Anna was showing signs of interest in inviting Jesus into her heart. In fact, her sister Caroline, my second granddaughter for whom we had also prayed daily, had invited Jesus into her heart on Thanksgiving day of 2000—a day she will always remember. When Melody told Anna about Caroline's decision, Anna responded that she was waiting to talk to her Nana. When this child came into the world, she gave me her heart. I feel as if she has chosen me. I don't understand it, but I am trying to handle her trust very carefully.

When Nana's "summer camp" was over, Anna stayed on with me for three additional days while her Mom and siblings returned to South Carolina. Here is my journal entry for Thursday, June 7, 2001:

"In my quiet time this morning, I was praying from the Anne Graham Lotz devotional book Daily Light—like the one I gave to Anna two years ago. I have been praying from this book with Anna on the phone every Thursday night for these past two years.

"The first scripture was Romans 10:9–10. Immediately, I felt the Holy Spirit remind me about Anna's need for Christ in her heart. So I asked God to give me just the right moment in the day to ask Anna if I could share with her how to ask Jesus into her heart.

That afternoon, the right moment came. I took her to Romans 3:23 and showed her our condition apart from Christ, His provision for us, and what our response could be. Then I asked her if she would like to ask Jesus into her heart. She smiled real big, and softly said 'Yes.' Then she prayed, confessing her sins and asking Jesus into her heart.

Of course, I cried. I said, 'Anna, you have been waiting for me to ask you about Jesus, haven't you?' Her eyes filled up with tears and her hug answered my question. She wrote these words in the margin of my Bible, next to Romans 10:9–10: 'I asked Jesus into my heart today—6/7/01.'"

What a sweet peace covered Anna the rest of the afternoon. There were many smiles! Our precious Anna is very private. I shared that we needed to tell her parents and her grandfather. She asked me to tell her parents and her Bop. That night, as we put her to bed, Bob prayed the sweetest prayer over Anna that any ear could hear. I know God's heart was touched, as was Anna's. What a humble experience—to be able to assist in showing Anna Christ's love for her.

As soon as I could, I called her parents. They also rejoiced. Her daddy said, "You could not have given me greater news in all the world today, and it seems so right that it was you, Nana! She loves you so much."

~

A month later I visited my then 94-year-old father and his wife. During the visit he handed me a letter he had written in his beautiful penmanship to Anna, expressing his joy in her decision to accept Christ and giving her verses of assurance to memorize. Someday in the future, Anna will show her child the handwritten letter she received from her great grandfather on her birthday in Christ.

♥ treasures of the heart

♥ Record the dates of your children's and grandchildren's salvation. Write down the day, the month, the year, and the season for each child. Record what you can remember about that child's experience. Then write a special prayer for this grandchild, thanking God for his or her salvation.

_____

_____

_____

_____

_____

_____

_____

_____

_____

_____

_____

_____

_____

_____

_____

_____

_____

_____

_____

_____

_____

_____

_____

_____

_____

_____

_____

_____

_____

_____

_____

_____

_____

_____

_____

_____

_____

_____

_____

pearls of wisdom

Start a new tradition: Each year, give your grandchildren an age-appropriate devotional book. Look for one in which he or she can journal. When you visit, ask your grandchild to share his or her writings with you.

"God Did It!"

It had been a busy day for Melody. Wednesdays were usually tough days—grocery shopping, a trip to the cleaners, and other excursions were scheduled on that day. But Wednesday afternoons were also Anna's favorite time of the week. Not yet in school but old enough for the preschool choir, this little one eagerly looked forward to her time at choir practice. She loved the teacher. She loved the music, she loved to sing, she loved the activities, and she loved the Bible stories. She always came home full of energy.

After bringing Anna home and giving her a cookie and milk, Melody was having difficulty settling Anna down for bed. She suggested that the two of them go upstairs and lie down on the bed for a few minutes to talk about choir practice.

"Tell Mommie what you learned in choir today, Anna," Melody said.

"Mother! Did you know that Jesus fed this huge crowd of people...and then His disciples gathered up the food, and there were just gobs left over?"

"How do you think that happened?" Melody asked.

Getting close to her mother's face, Anna said in a loud whisper, "God did it!"

What a wonderful truth! I'm so thankful for little children. They often preach powerful messages through child-like awe. Don't you love it when the breath of God brushes your heart with His words...painted by a child's simplicity?

"God can do anything, you know—far more than you could ever imagine or guess or request in your wildest dreams! He does it not by pushing us around but by working within us, his Spirit deeply and gently within us."

(Ephesians 3:20, THE MESSAGE)

♥ treasures of the heart

♥ Think back through your life to recall moments when you absolutely knew that "God did it!" Write about those experiences. Then write a prayer of thanks for God's faithfulness. Future generations may read your words and rejoice.

_____

_____

_____

_____

_____

_____

_____

_____

_____

_____

_____

_____

_____

_____

_____

_____

_____

_____

_____

_____

_____

_____

_____

_____

_____

_____

_____

_____

_____

_____

_____

❤ Begin a "Life Story Book" for your children and grandchildren. Purchase a small scrapbook and gather a few significant photos, such as your wedding day, your college graduation, your first house, or your first car. Begin slowly to write your life story. Take it one decade at a time, such as ages 1–10, 11–20, 21–30, 31–40, and so on, so you won't be overwhelmed.

Don't panic. It has taken a long time to live your life, and it will take a long time to write about it. Share this book with your grandchildren when they come to visit. Your children and your grandchildren will treasure having this written record of your life!

pearls of wisdom

⬤ With today's technology, most grandparents can operate a video camera. Take regular video shots of you and granddad—by yourselves, with your children, and with your grandchildren. Pass along these videos as a recorded history of your family.

⬤ Once in a while, visit a children's choir rehearsal at your church, just to enjoy watching and listening to the children and their teacher. Ask permission first, of course. And if you have a mind to do so, you might even bring some homemade cookies as a special "grandmother's treat."

⬤ Consider volunteering to help out with a children's choir. You will remind the children of their grandmothers. You may even get to be an "adopted grandmother" to a child. Bring along Granddad some days, too!

Do You Know Someone Who Is Hurting?

A pastor was visiting in a church member's home. He began to sense turmoil in the family, and asked God for a word or thought that he might share to help them begin talking to one another.

"Do you know anyone who is hurting today?" he asked.

Beth quickly responded: "I do! My daddy is hurting, but he doesn't want anyone to know it." She ran to her father, put her arms around his neck, and hugged him.

"Beth, stop it!" her father protested. "You're hugging me to death!"

"No, Daddy!" she replied, "I'm hugging you to life!"

~

All families struggle in their relationships. It's a common occurrence. These struggles never end! That's just part of being a family. How hard it is for children in a family when they sense hurt, or are themselves hurting.

But I know a secret: Nothing heals hurt more quickly than a touch. If it's true that people need eight hugs a day to be healthy, then you and I had better get busy! Can you recall a time when words just would not come or dare be spoken because the hurt was so deep? But then you felt someone's touch, and the hurt was released. That simple touch felt like a "hug to life."

~

In the spring of 2001 our daughter-in-love, our son's wife Colleen, had minor surgery on her knee. She came home with her knee bandaged, and had to walk on crutches. At first her daughter Milligan was afraid, and would not even come near. But after a little while she reached out and ever so gently touched her mother's knee, saying, "Mommie has big booboo." She then leaned down and kissed her mommie's knee.

The "touch of healing" can be a powerful tool. It is not used nearly enough in this day and age! As grandmothers, we have the power, time, and right to be regularly touching our children and grandchildren: affirming them, complimenting them, encouraging them, supporting them, and—most important—loving them to life!

♡ treasure in a box

Our tradition began when our children were young, to embrace each other in a huddle. The formula is simple: to scrunch up your shoulders, lean your head sorta' sideways, huddle close and enthusiastically sing "Hm-m-m-huh." "Hm-m-m-huh." When the family is all together, one person can yell at any time, "I feel a huddle coming on." We drop what we are doing and rush to join in and do just that.

∽

—*"GiGi" Stuart Calvert*

♥ treasures of the heart

♥ When was the last time you gave someone a "hug to life?" Our grandchildren need us to hug them, to touch them, and to let them know how special they are. Hugs can be phone calls, too. Give a hug today.

♥ Remember when you hugged a grandchild and kissed away the pain? Write about this event, and describe how that child responded to your comfort.

_____

_____

_____

_____

_____

_____

_____

_____

_____

_____

_____

_____

_____

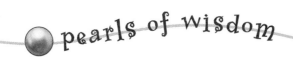

pearls of wisdom

Read Matthew 9:18–30. In your journal, write about these events in your own words. How did Jesus touch? What happened when he did?

_____

_____

_____

_____

_____

_____

_____

_____

_____

_____

_____

_____

_____

_____

_____

_____

_____

_____

_____

pearls of wisdom

You can "touch" a grandchild today: Send a funny card. Make a phone call. Or send an email. You can also send an "e-card." Log on to the Internet and go to one of several electronic e-card websites. One of my favorites is www.bluemountain.org. You can choose a card and then write your own text! And it's free! Your grandchildren will love getting an e-card from their grandmother—who even knows how to use the Internet! If you don't know how to do this, ask around—there's bound to be someone in your circle of friends who can teach you.

6

Building Lifelong Traditions

In 1999 I learned of Anne Graham Lotz's wonderful devotional book, *Daily Light*. The book is based on a classic Christian book by Samuel Bagster, first published in the 1790s. I was especially touched by Anne's story in the preface:

> Winning a relay race depends not only on the speed of the runners but also on their skillful ability to transfer the baton....
>
> In my family, one way the "baton" has been passed from generation to generation is through the use of the little volume entitled *Daily Light*...
>
> My grandmother gave a volume to my mother when she was a young child in China. ...My mother gave me my first volume on my tenth birthday. ...I gave a volume to my children on their tenth birthdays, and it has become a regular part of their daily devotions.

I thought about the blessing of all the family members reading the same scripture every day. *Daily Light* has morning and evening readings. It is simply Scripture—nothing else. I can't tell you how it ministers to my heart every day in my private prayer time.

Then I had an idea: Why not begin a "Burroughs family tradition" using *Daily Light*! I wrote to the author, Anne—who is also a good friend—telling her that I wanted to adopt her tradition of giving her children the book on their tenth birthday. I asked if she would be so kind as to autograph a book for each of my five grandchildren and one for each of their mothers. She was delighted to do this for me.

I gave Anna Esther the first copy in the summer of 1998, and presented one each to my daughter, Melody, and my daughter-in-love, Colleen. In the summer of 2001 I presented Caroline with her copy during a family worship time at Nana's Summer Camp. Three signed books now sit in my study, waiting for each of the last three grandchildren to turn ten.

Every Thursday that it is convenient to do so, I call Anna and Caroline on the phone. After a bit of conversation, I ask how I can pray for them. We read one of the daily verses together and then I pray for them—specifically and by name. Imagine how this tradition will bind our hearts to God and to each other!

Some day, when I am much older and Anna is in college, I hope my phone will ring on a Thursday night about 8:00 P.M. and she will say, "Nana, did you read the verse for today in *Daily Light*? Didn't you just love what it said! Nana, how can I pray for you today?"

I call this "passing on a legacy of faith." The psalmist says, *"And even when I am old and gray, O God, do not forsake me, until I declare Thy strength to this generation"* (Psalm 71:18).

You can do this, too. All it takes is a bit of time—and you have that. It takes a weekly phone call—and what grandmother would not want to speak to a grandchild weekly? And it takes a prayerful heart for each grandchild.

"Jacqueline prays like I do—on her knees. Her little fingers trace my wanderings and she tells God where I am. I tell all five how much I love them everyday!"

—*Barbara "Baby" Joiner*

♥ treasures of the heart

♥ Call your local Christian bookstore today to order *Daily Light*, by Samuel Bagster and Anne Graham Lotz. Start this tradition. The secret is wonderfully simple: a grandmother, a mother, and a grandchild, all reading the same scripture on the same day.

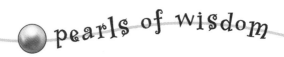

pearls of wisdom

You may want to give this book to a grand-child the Christmas before he or she turns ten, at a family reunion, or on that child's tenth birthday. Make it a special ceremony and cele-bration. You can do this by having a time of singing, and then read Anne's story from the preface. Have a special prayer and then present the signed book to this grandchild. Assure the other grandchildren that they also will receive this book when they turn ten.

Start a tradition by giving each grandchild an age-appropriate devotional book each year. This makes a great Christmas stocking gift. Look for a devotional in which they can journal. When you are visiting in their home, ask if you can share thoughts together and see how each of you is doing.

The "Price" of Peace

My daughter's family recently received a wonderful Christmas gift from friends. This handmade book, entitled *The Jesse Tree*, explains the symbols of our spiritual heritage and the different names we have for Jesus. Each of these names is attached to the pages of the book with velcro, and as each day's ritual of prayer and Bible reading is completed, the symbol is placed on the Christmas tree. This is a delightful way to help children and grandchildren learn the names of Jesus as you count down the days until December 25th (read Isaiah 11:1).

On one of my Christmas visits to my daughter's home I had the opportunity to participate in a "Jesse Tree" time of worship with her and my three granddaughters. It was Anna's turn to read, Caroline's turn to pray, and Frances' turn to place the symbol on the felt tree that hung in the entryway. Grandmothers really understand the significance of whose turn it is to do what! It was a beautiful moment in worship, and I cherished my daughter's attention to spiritual training and traditions with her girls and my grandgirls.

The second evening was still just the women folk. It was Caroline's turn to sit in Nana's lap and to read. Anna, the oldest, was on the floor with her own book, rolling her eyes and complaining that this would take too long because Caroline was a beginning reader.

The littlest one, Frances, was on the floor by me, misbehaving as she kept swinging her legs and hitting Caroline each time. Caroline complained, but kept reading, and I tried to reach down and grab hold of Frances's leg, but always missed! Melody warned Frances to stop, but she kept right on kicking. Suddenly, Melody grabbed Frances and headed upstairs. Though we could all hear Frances's cries, Caroline never hesitated. Pronouncing each word slowly, she read:

"His name shall be called Wond-er-ful
...Coun—Coun-sel-or...
Mighty God...Price of Peace!"

My heart skipped a beat! I did not correct her. In the middle of a somewhat less-than-peaceful family altar, amidst the chaos of one grandchild getting a spanking, another acting indifferent and impatient, and one in my lap struggling to pronounce the words, I heard God whisper: Yes, He *is* the *priceless* Prince of Peace! His life brings peace to our chaos.

I find myself looking more and more these days for those "ah-ha" moments, when I am able to see God in all His glory: stooping down, in my chaos, and allowing His own Son, the Price of Peace, to become flesh. God *"became flesh and blood, and moved into the neighborhood,"* forever touching our everyday lives with His peace (John 1:14, THE MESSAGE). That gift, dear reader, was given at a very great price.

*"When you can't alter
the whirling pace,
retire to your inner sanctuary
and alter yourself."*

—*Charlie Shedd,*
How to Make People Really Feel Loved

♥ treasures of the heart

♥ Find a copy of the book, *Two From Galilee*, by Marjorie Holmes. Perhaps there is one in your church library. Fix yourself a cup of tea and invite some peace into your life by enjoying this delightful story. So it's not Christmas! His peace is ours. It is everlasting. And it is for all seasons.

♥ If your grandchild is a preteen, introduce him or her to the book *Two From Galilee*. It is easy reading and will make for great dialogue for the two of you. If convenient, read it aloud together

♥ While at a bookstore, browse holiday books and glean ideas for your next holiday. Go ahead, make a morning of it. Grab a cup of special coffee or even lunch at the bookstore, and settle in to just read. Pamper yourself!

♥ Give a copy of *The Jesse Tree*, by Raymond and Georgene Anderson, to your children to help them encourage their children to learn about Jesus' names.

A good book is a lifelong friend

♥ My favorite books:

_____

_____

_____

_____

_____

♥ My grandchild's favorite books:

_____

_____

_____

_____

_____

"If you are too busy to read, you are too busy."

~

—*Richard Foster, author*

pearls of wisdom

● Call another grandmother and invite her to tea this week. Over tea or coffee, share this book with her and help her to begin a tradition with her grandchildren.

● Pray this prayer for a grandchild:

Father, my heart is so full of the treasures of my grandchildren. Today I ask your divine protection and care as _____ goes to school. May he/she be made aware of You in someone's kindness toward him/her, or in making a new friend, or in a kind word from a special teacher. I pray this prayer in the strong name of Your Son Jesus. Amen.

Praying for Our Grandchildren

The grandparenting journey has been wonderful for Bop and me, and we pray daily for our grandchildren. Through the years we have had many anxious phone calls from our children, asking for specific prayers for their children—our grandchildren. I can still feel the tug of pain we felt as we prayed for each family need.

When we pray, we must learn to "leave it there," just as the old gospel song tells us. Early in the morning, on my knees, I often take my children and grandchildren to the Lord, praying scripture over each of their lives. At about noon, I go back and pick up where I left off. The reason I know I pick it back up is that I begin to ponder it again. …Well, to be honest, I begin to worry about it again. Not only that: I begin to explain to God just how I want those prayers answered!

∼

"Pray" is a four letter word
that you can say anywhere.

∼

—Unknown

Earl Lee, in his book *The Cycle of Victorious Living*, describes a way of life and prayer based on selected verses from Psalm 37.

～

Delight yourself in the LORD and he will give you the desires of your heart.

Commit your way to the LORD;
trust in Him and He will do this:

He will make your righteousness shine like the dawn,
the justice of your cause like the noonday sun.

Be still before the LORD and wait patiently before him. (vv. 4–7)

～

Here's how it works:

Step One: I commit my cares to the Lord. I take my problem, whatever it is, and figuratively lay it out on my hands, my palms facing upward. I specifically state what it is, then I turn my hands down—with my palms open, and let the problem drop into God's hand. I commit the problem to Him.

Psalm 37 instructs us to commit our way to the Lord. Then immediately it tells us to trust Him. Now I have relinquished my problem to the Lord.

Step Two: I begin to trust God with what I have given Him. By an act of faith, not feelings,

I say "Thank you, Lord, for I know You are taking care of my problem. Lord, I believe. Help my unbelief."

Step Three: I delight myself in the Lord. I praise Him and thank Him for what He can and will do.

Step Four: Rest in the Lord.

You have committed your care to God. You are trusting in Him. You delight in Him. Now you are called to rest in Him.

Surrendering is hard to do. By nature, we want to fix things ourselves. We want to play God—we think we know best. What foolishness!

The psalmist tells us to "be still before the Lord." Rest. You have committed your cares to the Lord. It is not in your power or control. What a comfort these words are!

∼

Here is an acrostic, based on the word delight, to help you remember these steps:

> **D**aily
> **E**verything
> **L**aid
> **I**nto
> **G**od's
> **H**ands
> **T**otally

Pray this prayer for your child or grandchild:

"'For I know the plans I have for

_____

(insert your grandchild's name),

declares the Lord. 'Plans to prosper you and not to harm you, plans to give you hope and a future.'" (NIV)

Scripture helps us see God's perspective. After all, this is God's breathed Word—His living Word. As Charles Spurgeon once said, "Prayer is the slender nerve that moves the muscles of omnipotence."

_____

_____

_____

_____

_____

_____

_____

_____

_____

_____

♡ treasures of the heart

♡ Begin praying in this manner for your children and your grandchildren. Even as I write these words I am reminded that for years I prayed this way for my children. Now I need to begin praying this way for my grandchildren.

_____

_____

_____

_____

_____

_____

_____

_____

_____

_____

_____

_____

_____

_____

_____

_____

_____

♥ treasures of the heart

♥ Claim Scripture verses for your children and grandchildren as you pray, inserting their names in the Bible passages. Use Psalm 8, for example.

_____

_____

_____

_____

_____

_____

_____

_____

_____

_____

_____

_____

_____

_____

_____

_____

_____

_____

_____

_____

_____

_____

_____

_____

_____

_____

_____

_____

_____

_____

_____

_____

_____

_____

_____

_____

_____

♥ God tells us *"Call to me and I will answer you and tell you great and unsearchable things you do not know"* (Jeremiah 33:3 NIV). If God is willing to do even more than we know, things beyond what we can even imagine or think, then we should be praying daily—even hourly—for our children and grandchildren.

pearls of wisdom

Often one of the most difficult things for the family to do is to pray together. Prayer is an intimate experience, which is all the more reason we should bind ourselves together in prayer as a family, praying for and with each other often. You, grandmother, can be the catalyst for family prayer time, if it is not already a regular occurrence in your family time. Be creative as to how you begin such an experience. Begin simply. It will catch on and become a precious time.

"I do think that families are the most beautiful things in all the world."

—*Jo March,*
Little Women

9

God "Wuvs" Us

*"We are all pencils in the hand
of a writing God, who is sending
love letters to the world."*

~

—Mother Teresa

Once, while walking past the grandchildren's bedroom, I noticed Anna, age two, on the floor reading to nine-month-old Caroline. I paused to listen.

Anna had her arms around Caroline's waist. She was holding their children's Bible, showing Caroline the pictures. Turning the pages slowly, she read, "God wuvs us." Next page: "God wuvs us." Next page: "God wuvs us."

As I watched this precious scene, I silently prayed. "Father, draw these children to Yourself with this simple truth: "God wuvs us!" *What a sermon!*

~

♥ treasures of the heart

♥ Consider someone in your "circle of influence" who might need to know "God Wuvs Us." Write a letter to that person, sharing God's love through scripture. Pray that your letter will help him or her receive the truth of John 3:1 and other "love" verses.

_____

_____

_____

_____

_____

_____

_____

_____

_____

_____

_____

_____

_____

_____

_____

_____

_____

_____

💜 Record in your journal a story of when your grandchildren have been a "living sermon" in your life. Thank God for this memory.

_____

_____

_____

_____

_____

_____

_____

_____

_____

_____

_____

_____

_____

_____

_____

_____

_____

_____

_____

_____

_____

_____

drawing by Anna, age 6

How Big Is God?

"Love that goes upward is worship.
Love that goes outward is affection.
Love that stoops is grace."

~

—*Chuck Swindoll*

On their way home from church, a child asked her mother, "Mommy, the preacher said that God is bigger than we are. Is that true?"

"Yes, that's true," her mother replied.

"He also said that God lives in us. Is that true, too?"

Again, the mother replied, "Yes."

"Well," pondered the little girl, "if God is bigger than we are, and He lives in us, wouldn't He show through?"

An inner-city child in a Houston missionary day-care facility said to the missionary, "Ms. Quarter, are you God?"

"No," Ms. Quarter replied, "but God's love lives in my heart."

"No! You **are** God!" the child insisted.

"No, I am not, but God's Son, Jesus, lives in my heart," persisted Ms. Quarter.

Pointing to Ms. Quarter's heart, the child said, "You **are** God, 'cause I can see Him right there!"

Can our grandchildren see God in us?
We should strive always to let God
show through us, modeling His love
for our grandchildren.

♥ treasures of the heart

♥ Call a local community service agency and ask if you can volunteer one afternoon. Take one of your grandchildren with you. Ask about their needs, and how the two of you might serve them.

♥ Plan a "God Showing through Us" day with your grandchildren—at an assisted living center, a church center, or at the Salvation Army—perhaps helping the children in one of these programs. Help in any way you are needed.

♥ Before you go, find out how many children are involved. Prepare a basket of goodies and surprises especially wrapped for them.

_____

_____

_____

_____

_____

_____

_____

_____

_____

_____

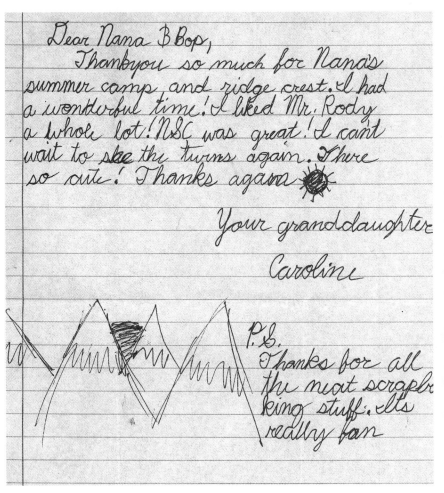

Dear Nana B Bop,

Thankyou so much for Nana's summer camp, and ridge crest. I had a wonderful time! I liked Mr. Rody a whole lot! NSC was great! I can't wait to see the twins again. There so cute! Thanks again.

Your granddaughter

Caroline

P.S.
Thanks for all the neat scrapbooking stuff. It's really fun

note from Caroline, age 10

Friends

"There is a friend
who sticks closer than a brother."

~

Proverbs 18:24 NIV

She had been warned many times, and was warned about what would happen if she was late one more time. But this little one's habit was always to be late. Begging for just one more chance, and promising to do better, she was allowed to play at Becky's house. Firmly she was warned that she was to be home at 4:30—on the dot!

But 4:30 came...and went. The clock showed 5:00. Then, at 5:15, the little one bounded through the door—all smiles and totally unaware of the trouble she was in. She walked right into her father, who had been standing at the door waiting for her return.

She looked up to see her father's face glaring down, and stopped dead in her tracks.

"You are in serious trouble, young lady. It is 5:15, and you are 45 minutes late. Do you have a good explanation?" he asked.

Looking up with her sweet innocent smile, she told her Daddy that Becky had dropped her doll and had broken it.

"I suppose you thought you needed to stay and fix it?" he said in his big Daddy voice.

"Oh no, Daddy! I just stayed to help her cry!"

"Where will the kind, thoughtful, caring people come from for the next generation—if our children are not taught the value of putting someone else's needs above their own?"

—*Edith Schaeffer*

treasures of the heart

♥ Write in your journal about a time in your childhood when you got into trouble, and the outcome. At some appropriate time, share this story with a grandchild. Your grandchild may begin to see you in a different light!

_____

_____

_____

_____

_____

_____

_____

_____

_____

_____

_____

_____

_____

_____

_____

♥ Plan a "Doll Tea Party" with one or all of your grandchildren. Send invitations and ask for an RSVP. Have old gloves, hats, purses, and hankies ready for each invited guest to wear at the party. Use a small table and chairs, if available. Have cookies and milk (or real tea). Be sure to take photos.

pearls of wisdom

⬤ Schedule a "Doll Repair Afternoon," when you and you granddaughter(s) do doll repairs and wash and iron doll clothes and blankets. This will be a good time for talking with them, when you will learn lots of new things. Be sure to take photos!

_____

_____

_____

_____

_____

_____

_____

_____

_____

_____

Friendship, At All Times

"A friend loves at all times."

~

Proverbs 17:17

The granddaughters had worked hard on their memory verses, to present at the conclusion of Nana's "Summer Camp." These memory skills were much easier for the two older girls because they were already in grade school and read well.

We worked every day on the memory verses, preparing to recite them for their parents on the last day of the camp. The time came! The parents sat in rapt attention. The stage was set.

Standing tall, from the oldest to the youngest, they began their memory-verse recitation. I watched as the youngest, Frances, drew herself up tall, swallowed hard, took a deep breath, and then recited clearly: "Love others at other times."

What a great paraphrase: "Love others...at other times"! This is so true—we should love others at *other* times...at *all* times...at *every* time.

Now, what can we learn and teach our grandchildren from Frances's wonderful paraphrase?

♥ treasures of the heart

♥ When your grandchildren are visiting and the time is right, share with them that friends don't just choose "the right times" to be friends, but that true friends choose to be friends *all* the time. Read them the book *Love You Forever* by Robert Munsch. This is a powerful children's book about parent-child love, and makes a great gift.

♥ Just for fun, send a handmade card about friendship to your grandchildren. Use construction paper and creative stickers. Put a surprise in each envelope, such as a bookmark, stickers, a stick of gum, or even a dollar bill.

● pearls of wisdom

● Rent the movie classic *A Secret Garden* to watch with your grandchildren. Pop plenty of popcorn, and allow time to discuss the movie afterwards. See what pearls of wisdom you can mine from the conversation.

_____

_____

_____

_____

In person, by email, or on the phone, tell your grandchildren why you would choose them as a friend. On this journal page, write the names of each of your children and grandchildren, beginning with the oldest, in order of age. Beside each name, list one or two enduring characteristics of each grandchild. Remember: This book will be passed down from generation to generation and will become a great blessing to them long after you are gone. It will thrill them to know that you recognized their sterling character traits.

Spill a Glass of Tea, Please

Bob and I had the privilege of sharing a great friendship with the late humorist and entertainer, Grady Nutt. Grady was the one who said, "I'm me, and that's good, 'cause God don't make no junk."

Grady was a guest in our home many times. He infected our family life with his sense of humor and wisdom. He taught me much about humor and its importance in life. He could wrap you around his finger with his laughter—all the while stuffing "life-changing gospel" into your heart and soul. He was a master storyteller, and could captivate his audience with great truths. I can still hear his deep laughter.

One of his stories has been pivotal for me and my family. The story happened somewhere out in West Texas. As was their tradition, several families met at Grandmother's house for a big Thanksgiving dinner celebration. They had gathered for years to eat that special meal, prepared with great love and care. This particular year, the family members realized that this might be the last Thanksgiving meal Grandmother would be able to prepare by herself. No one wanted to miss it—just thinking about the feast made their mouths water.

All the preparations had been made, with the traditional decorations and the special menu. The table was set with the special linen tablecloth and napkins. The china, crystal, and sterling silver were in their proper places. By now, everyone had access to Grandmother's secret recipes...yet they still tasted better when served at her table. According to tradition, everyone knew exactly where he or she would sit. Even the little ones got to sit at the "big table" for this event. It was a sacred hour, indeed.

As tradition dictated, everyone around the table joined hands while Grandpa said grace for the meal. Each person bowed his or her head as the prayer was offered. As Grandpa finished the prayer and they all released hands, the little grandson sitting next to Grandpa reached out his hand and somehow knocked over his glass of tea. The tea stain began to slowly move past the green beans, past the mashed potatoes, and on toward the carrots.

The entire family gasped as they turned their heads toward Grandmother. After a few moments of uncomfortable silence, Grandpa pronounced, "It appears to me that this is too heavy a burden for a little fellow to carry all by himself!" With that remark, he reached out and knocked over *his* tea glass!

Once again, a collective gasp of disbelief was heard as Grandpa's tea moved down the middle of the table—past the turkey, the dressing, the rolls, and on toward the salad, heading right for Grandmother. Every eye turned to Grandmother and then back to Grandpa—back and forth as if in a tennis match. Then, looking down the long table at Grandpa, Grandma shouted, "Me too!" and knocked over *her* glass of tea!

Laughter and tears mingled together at a family celebration that would never be forgotten —when a grandchild's life was forever engraved in grace.

"It's a good thing to have the props pulled out from under us occasionally. It gives us some sense of what is rock under our feet, and what is sand."

~

—*Madeleine L'Engle,*
The Summer of the Great-Grandmother

♥ treasures of the heart

♥ Next Thanksgiving, plan a special worship celebration to immediately follow the meal. Involve all the grandchildren in the planning and in the service itself. Here is a suggested order:

Hymn: *"We Gather Together"*

Scripture: _____ (an older grandchild)

Prayer: (a younger grandchild)

Testimony Time: Go around the room and let each person tell the most meaningful thing about Thanksgiving— what this time together means, something special about the meal, or what he or she is thankful for.

Prayer of Celebration: (a grandfather or father)

Chorus: *"God Is So Good"*

Devotional Thought: (one of the older grandchildren or a mom)

Prayer: (another adult)

♥ treasure in a box

I drove up to the bank window and handed the teller a check that I had written to my eleven-year-old granddaughter, Anna. I gave the check to the teller with my driver's license and said, "This is my granddaughter, Anna. Her father is a vice president of this bank, and I would like to cash this check." The teller nodded and promptly cashed the check. It worked. I used Anna's father's name and position to accomplish my task.

When you pray for your grandchildren, use your Father's name and position to lay claim to His promises. He has given you His name (John 14:13).

A Prayer of Grace

Spring, 2000

Dear Bob,

You have had an important place in my daughter Amy's life. God has used you in a unique way to minister to her and encourage her spirit. I will always remember your phone call to my office from Palm Beach Atlantic College, asking where Amy was and why she was withdrawing from school. Your call to her that day—your counsel and encouragement—was the reason she decided to stay in school. Then, through that year, you continued to be her own personal cheerleader, lifting her up and allowing her to believe in herself. She told us several times of your encouragement, hugs, faith in her, and help as she faced decisions. I sometimes wonder if you even knew how much you did for her by just being who you are.

Then, lastly, you took time away from your vacation trip to New York City to see her in the Broadway production of *Cats*. Your presence validated who she was, and that she was good enough to make it. All through these last four years, while she has been on the road with *Cats*, you've never failed to ask about her and send her your love and encouragement.

There are no words to express to you how full this papa's heart is for all you have done. You are one of four persons whom God, the Father, has used to answer the prayers of Valerie and me. Men and women of God helped form who Amy is. I will forever be in your debt.

I have told your precious Esther how grateful I am for you, and that the only way I could begin to repay you is to pray continually for you and for her, for your children, and especially for your grandchildren.

You see, Bob, God placed you in Amy's life because I asked Him to do so. When Amy was 11 and Matt was 8, God placed on my heart a burden for the men and women who would have a profound influence on their lives. I prayed that God would send people into their lives that were Christ-like, God-serving, compassionate, and full of grace—at just the right time, He has answered my prayer over and over again by placing "Bobs" like you to guide them, to teach by example, and to love them through the growing times of their lives.

So here, along with the names of the children and grandchildren of seven other important people who have influenced my kids, I add your name, Esther's name, and the names of your children and grandchildren to my prayer list. I pray often that God, the Father, will provide for each of them godly men and women who will guide and love them in their walk toward Christ, and that He will provide for your family the same compassionate and loving encouragement and hope that you've placed into the life of one of my most precious children, His child Amy.

Please share this with Esther.

Thanks again, Bob, for making yourself available to be used of God.

Always your friend,
Dick Hamel

*"If only God will enable me
to tend to the possible, depending
on Him for the impossible."*

—*Ruth Bell Graham,*
It's My Turn

♥ treasures of the heart

♥ Who was one of the most influential people in your life? Can you recall that person's name? Write that name in your journal and, if possible, write that person a letter—thanking them for their influence in your life. For the cost of a stamp you can bless someone abundantly.

_____

_____

_____

_____

_____

_____

_____

_____

_____

_____

_____

_____

_____

_____

_____

_____

💜 Begin praying now that God will place just the right person in the lives of your grandchildren—at just the right time to help them walk with God. It doesn't matter the ages of your grandchildren—just pray often for them and for those who will influence them.

💜 Write a note to one of your grandchildren's teachers, promising your prayers and giving an encouraging scripture or quote. This will bless the teacher and be a powerful witness.

_____

_____

_____

_____

_____

_____

_____

_____

_____

_____

_____

_____

_____

_____

pearls of wisdom

🔘 Consider asking a friend with grandchildren to covenant with you to pray daily for each other's grandchildren, Stay in touch with each other by email or phone so you will know how to pray specifically. This will lead to celebrating answered prayers together, and mutual support through troubling times as well.

🔘 Consider "adopting" the child of a single parent. Share with the parent that you would like to pray for the child and to be an "adopted grandmother." If allowed to do this, make sure to communicate often with the child by note-card, email, or phone. Ever so often, take the child for ice cream or for a walk in the park.

🔘 Choose the child or children of one of your missionary friends and adopt him or her in daily prayer. Write him or her frequent letters.

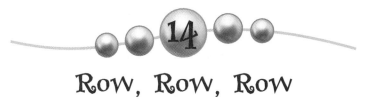

Row, Row, Row Your Boat

Our son David and his wife Colleen have a wonderful tradition with their twins, Milligan and Walker. After the evening meal is completed and the table is cleared, they sit together as a family and sing. The children love the fun, action-songs such as "Row, row, row your boat gently down the steam." Eventually they move to the familiar "Allelu, Allelu, Allelu, Alleluia! Praise ye the Lord." As Walker sings the last "Pwaise ye the Lord," he throws his head back, opens his little mouth, and slides up an octave as he sings the last note!

While observing this grand event on a visit, I watched their granddad, Bop, smiling as he listened with great delight. When they finished singing the last line, Walker reached out and grabbed Bop's arm, saying in a loud voice, "Pwaise ye the Lord, Bop!" Immediately Bop joined in the singing.

Following this time of singing, it is then story time, bath time, and finally prayer time. Each parent holds a child as they name all the cousins, aunts, uncles, grandparents, friends, and even Maddi the dog. Their prayer time also ends with singing.

On this particular night, Walker led out with "Jesus loves me." Colleen then invited Milligan to choose a song. In her deep voice, Milligan began, "Row, row, row your boat." We all joined in, and I smiled, grateful that Bop and I were a part of this tradition.

Later, I reflected on the experience and realized that some days are truly "Jesus Loves Me" days. And then there are "Row, row, row your boat" days! As a grandmother, I am grateful for the "Jesus loves me" days, but I am also aware that Jesus spent time in boats, calming the sea and inviting His friends to get out of the boat. I am glad that Jesus, who loves me, has such great knowledge of His father's care that He could sleep through the storm. In or out of the boat, He is with us.

So have a great "Pwaise ye the Lord" day! Break out in song! You will find that the melody stays in your heart all day long.

sent by Milligan and Walker, age 2

♥ treasures of the heart

♥ Singing is a great tradition to have with your family—large or small. Begin early having music in the family times. You can't beat Mozart in the background of conversation, meals, or fellowship times!

♥ Buy a child's Scripture/song cassette tape or CD. Give it to your grandchildren for their next car trip. You will be mentoring them in God's words and truth. Singing Scripture songs helps children memorize the Scriptures and puts them deep in their hearts. You can find these at most bookstores.

♥ If you have teenage grandkids, select such albums as "Point of Grace," anything by Steven Curtis Chapman, 4 Him, and others. The bookstore can help you with Christian teen favorites.

♥ The next time you are with your grandkids in the car, sing together, no matter how it sounds! Teach them your favorite childhood songs. They will enjoy hearing songs that you sang as a child.

Dear Nana and Bop

I am fine. I hope you are to.
Carline is fine But Frances
on the other hand is being
I ven the terebel she has
ton quite a lot not cont-
ing the other things. I
kelly ingoy Being whit
you. P.S.
        I Love you.
        Oh Look at the
time
        I have to go
        Love
          Anna

note from Anna, age 7

86

16

Nana's Summer Camp

Since the early summer of 1998, I've had what has become known as "Nana's Summer Camp." I borrowed the idea from church friends whose grandparents had done this kind of camp for years. I only have five grandchildren—and they live miles apart. I want my children and my grandchildren to know and enjoy each other, so I plan the camp. All they have to do is show up!

Each year, camp has a theme scripture and a theme song. I begin sending the grandchildren hints about the camp theme in January. They love to try to figure out the theme. We also send menus with crazy meal choices:

Breakfast (check one)
　__ milk
　__ orange juice
　__ flavored swamp-water

Lunch (check one)
　__ peanut butter and jelly sandwich
　__ ham 'n cheese sandwich
　__ gator tail sandwich

Dinner (check one)
　__ macaroni & cheese
　__ spaghetti
　__ fish eyes on wild rice

Each grandchild marks his menu choices and mails it back. I give them a "thumbs-up" on bringing their American Girls dolls and/or teddy bears for the tea party day. I also ask them to bring their own special videos.

Bob and I begin to prepare months ahead. I purchase items throughout the year, all age-appropriate. In early spring, we prepare and send the Official Nana's Summer Camp Brochure (produced on our computer)—stating the theme and announcing some of the activities we will be doing at camp. Of course, there are always "Nana Surprises"—two times a day. Cardinal Rule: You may switch surprises, but no complaining allowed!

Admission to Nana's Summer Camp is "one hug and four kisses" from each grandchild, payable upon arrival at the camp front door. As they enter the front door for camp, each child finds his or her room assignment listed on the kitchen cabinet—along with the Camp Rules. The list of rules must be signed by each camper.

Camp Rules 2000:

1. First-time obedience!
2. First-time manners!
3. First-time splash into bed!
4. Splash out and put back all stuff!
5. Splash quickly to snack time!
6. Splash hard and memorize scripture!
7. SPLASH FUN over all campers!
8. All together now—Let's make a Splash!!

Twice a day we have snacks—one of their favorite times.

At the 2001 camp, I put an old sheet on the kitchen table and gave each grandchild a box of glitter glue paint. Each child painted a corner of the sheet to their hearts' delight. (Oops! I forgot to put "paint shirts" on the painters and ruined one good camp T-shirt!) Each child painted something related to the camp theme. We put the camp mural on the patio to dry, and the next day we put it back on the table. It hung over the table to the floor, making a "tent" where they hid to have their snacks. Simple fun!

Each day, camp includes
- a Bible story
- Bible memory verses
- a Missionary Moment
- a field trip
- water sports
- crafts
- rest time (the favorite time for adults)
- surprises
- jacuzzi or pool fun
- lots of touching and hugging

The grandchildren have come to love the Missionary Moments. In preparation for NSC (Nana's Summer Camp), I email five missionaries in five areas of the world, and assign one grandchild to each missionary. I ask the missionaries for prayer needs and ask them to send me an email about their work. Some of them even send pictures to download! We print them out and have them available on the day they are to be our prayer focus. The grandchildren love this part, and it helps them visualize where the missionaries serve.

I place a large, laminated map of the world on the glass kitchen tabletop. This stays in place all week under a plastic tablecloth, as this is also where we do crafts each day. For the Missionary Moment, I remove the tablecloth and we gather around the kitchen table. Each day, a child reads the missionary letter and shows the photos. Everyone tries to find the country and city where the missionary family lives and serves. When the place is found, a sticker in placed on the map. We then hold hands and pray for the missionary, their family, and their ministry.

What missionaries or mission fields are dear to you? How can you plant a missionary seed in your grandchildren's hearts?

_____

_____

_____

_____

_____

_____

Our second year of Nana's Summer Camp, the twins, Milligan and Walker, were 18 months old. As you might imagine, they loved the "sticker" part. The twins stayed an extra day. The next morning, I discovered Milligan climbing up to the kitchen table, pushing back the tablecloth, and reaching in to get the stickers. She looked over to see me watching her. (She knows she is not allowed on the table!) When I saw what she was doing, I ran to get more stickers and gave them to her. She pushed the cloth back some more. I watched as she placed a sticker on the map, and then clapped her hands in delight. She then folded her hands as if to pray—a "holy moment" for this Nana.

Precious grandmothers, we must pass on our legacy of faith to the next generation. If I do no other thing in their lives than teach them how important it is to pray for missionaries, I will have blessed another generation.

Nana's Summer Camp Schedule

Wednesday
Afternoon arrival
Welcome
Nana and Bop
Activities
Swim/relax
Orientation
Dinner: Mexican stack-ups
Hang-out time/story time
Beds/clothes/surprises (can't grumble/can
    exchange)

Thursday
8:00: Breakfast
8:30: Bible story
Missionary Moment
Memory verse
Activity: Museum/lunch
Rest Time: video/books
Activity: Scrap booking with the older girls
Twins: swim, art/legos
Late-afternoon swim
Dinner: Chicken casserole/fruit salad
Worship service
Sweat shirts painting
Bath and story time

Friday
8:00: Breakfast
8:30: Bible story
Missionary Moment
Activity: Water slide/games/crafts
Lunch: Peanut butter & jelly or turkey sandwiches
Rest Time: Video
Activity: Movie with the older girls
Twins: Video with Nana
Dinner: Nana's world-famous spaghetti with
    tossed salad and asiago cheese bread

Saturday
8:30: Bible story
Missionary Moment
9:00 Breakfast: Krispy Kreme
Surprise trip and picnic lunch
Rest Time: Video
Activity: Bake and deliver cookies to neighbors
Cookies/ice cream stuff
Water games
Dinner: Chicken/green salad

Sunday
8:30: Breakfast
Bible Story
Missionary Moment
Activity: Final rehearsal for camp program
The Camp Finale ! ! ! !
CAMP ENDS!!!

♥ treasures of the heart

♥ It's never too late to begin a Nana's Summer Camp! It will be a great experience for you and your grandchildren! Make up your own schedule or follow and improve on the one above. It can be as long or as short as you want it to be. And it can be as simple or elaborate as you wish. Just do it!

"Nana's Summer Camp was outstanding. Thank you, Mom, for the hours of prep work that went into our time together. You'll probably never fully realize the impact that your NSC tradition is having on our girls. Thank you for doing it!"

—Melody Burroughs Reid, June 2001

The Oil of Joy

We started a "Burroughs tradition" in 1998. Bob and I rent a wonderful beach house for the Labor Day weekend and invite our adult children and our grandchildren to join us. We pay for it—they come! We design this to be a time of fun: games, beach, ice cream cones, tennis, biking, swimming, eating—everyone doing whatever they wish to do. The purpose of this tradition is to make sure our grandchildren grow up together—making life-long memories. It also turns out to be a good time to celebrate the birthdays of all the grandchildren.

Traditionally, when the Burroughs family gathers for any extended time, we try to have a time of worship and celebration. On the most recent Labor Day weekend, Bob and I were especially excited. Our son-in-love, Will, and our daughter-in-love, Colleen, had recently been asked by their respective churches to serve as deacons. We decided that our worship time on this retreat would honor these family members.

Bob usually plans our worship times, giving each of us a specific responsibility. The Reid girls helped him plan this service. He assigned them the task of presenting "symbols of a servant lifestyle." Bob read John 13, the story of Jesus washing the feet of His disciples, teaching them to serve each other.

After singing a hymn, Bob spoke to Will and Colleen about their new responsibility of service. He asked them to kneel behind the coffee table. Immediately, our little grandson, Walker, dropped to his knees, folding his hands together shyly in front of his mother. This was an "ahhh" moment!

Then our oldest granddaughter, Anna, took a Bible and laid it in front of them, saying, "This is God's Word and your guide as a servant." Caroline, the next oldest, brought a towel and said, "This towel is a symbol of a servant lifestyle." Frances, the youngest Reid granddaughter, brought a basin, representing the water that Jesus used to prepare His disciples for service.

Bob then anointed the foreheads of Colleen and Will with the "Oil of Joy," invoking a blessing over their new ministry. Each member of the families was invited to come and offer a blessing or pray over Colleen and Will. I watched as Melody bent over her husband to pray for him. A lump formed in my throat, and joy flooded my heart. What a picture for my grandchildren to see!

What happened next was the breath of God touching our family. Milligan stood up, crossed the room, and picked up her plastic crayon container. She then gave one of her crayons to her mother and then to her Uncle Will. Our tears were our final prayer. The twins reminded us afresh of the power of kneeling and blessing!

Isaiah tells us that a little child shall lead us. In Proverbs 20:11, we find these words: *"Even a child is known by his actions, by whether his conduct is pure and right"* (NIV).

~

Grandmothers, no one could have planned what happened in our time of worship that day! It was a God thing! I do know this: events like this will probably never happen unless we grandparents plan opportunities for God to bless our family times together. I beg you—pass on your godly heritage of faith. Build in worship memories for your family.

"Ma's standing in a chair, listening to Christian radio and singing the hymns. She does it every afternoon. It's her joy!"

~

—*Grandpa Milligan, 1935*

♡ treasures of the heart

♡ Family worship ideas can be found in a variety of places, such as in books, magazines, and through research on the Internet. Ask your pastor or another church staff member to help you finding resources for planning a family worship celebration.

♡ The earlier you begin times of family worship, the easier it will be to maintain the tradition. And regardless of how your teen grandchildren feel about it, do it anyway! They will come to appreciate it and will fondly recall these times when they are more mature.

♡ Think back on a favorite family worship time—either a growing-up time or a present family time—and journal your thoughts and comments for future generations to read.

♡ Visit a Christian bookstore. You will find many wonderful age-appropriate devotional books that you can share with your grandchildren. I challenge you to plan a time of worship the next time your grandchildren will be with you: the whole family together, right after mealtime, or just you and a grandchild before bedtime.

We are enjoying our grandparenting—with all 13 of our grandchildren—each one special! One thing I have done is write a personal letter to each of our grandchildren, usually the week after they are born. I mention something of what the world was like at the time they were born, how we have been praying for their arrival, something about their parents and the anticipated joy they have for them, and then something about Marilynn and me, and our pledge to pray for them daily, to be available for them as they grow, and how special they are to us. I then give each of them a carefully chosen and prayed-over scripture just for them. The parents especially really treasure this letter for Grandpa and Grandma Blackaby.

Marilynn then makes an heirloom dress for each of the girls, and makes something special for each of the boys. We also have been planning and implementing a family gathering of our five children and their families every other year, so the cousins can get to know and love each other.

~

Henry & Marilynn Blackaby

Nanny's Blessing

In the last video of the *Jesus the One and Only* series, Beth Moore tells a wonderful grandmother story. She has given me permission to share it with you.

As a five-year-old child, Beth had a fall so bad that the impact pushed her baby teeth up in her mouth—causing her baby teeth to turn black. She could hardly wait for those ugly teeth to come out so her permanent teeth would grow in pearly white.

As Beth describes it,

"Pearly white they were, but they had been pushed up, and when they came in they grew out of the front of my mouth! Now, do you understand what I'm saying? I'm not talking 'buck teeth!' I'm talking teeth you could set your sandwich on—and save it for later. And in those days, for whatever excruciating reason, they made you live with your teeth like that before they would fix them. And all the while, your self-esteem is suffering in ways you can't imagine. Kids are so cruel....

"I'm telling the truth. At that particular time, I could not put my lips together! No matter what I did, my teeth would not come together.

I had a third-grade class picture coming up. You know—the kind they take with the blue background?

"And I told my mom, 'I'm not having my picture taken!'

"She said, 'You are most certainly are! You are so beautiful to us.'

"I stood in the bathroom and literally practiced putting my lips together until my teeth were sore and my lips were raw. I wasn't even trying to smile. I just simply wanted to cover them up. At that time, I constantly held my left hand over my mouth. It was traumatic for me.

"So the day came for the picture. I went and stood in front of the camera and I had my hand over my mouth. The gentleman said, 'You're going to have to put your hand down, honey.'

"I said, 'Are you ready to take the picture? Count to three and I will put my hand down.' He counted...one...two...three, and I dropped my hand. He took the picture. I walked away, thinking *I did it...that wasn't so bad*. Until about six weeks later, when the teacher brought in a stack of pictures. My heart was pounding. When she laid it down on my desk, I lay on top of the picture—trying to cover it up. My classmates made fun by calling me names.

"When I walked home that day, my mother

and my grandmother, my 'Nanny,' were standing in the kitchen. I said, 'Don't you ever make me do anything like that again.' I took those pictures and tore them up and threw them in the trash. I was devastated, and I guess they were, too. All those years went by. I wore braces for 12 solid years. That's how long it took to fix that mouth.

"My precious Nanny passed away when I was 16. I was in my early twenties and was visiting in my mother's house in another city. We were visiting together and she said, 'You're not gonna believe what I found the other day!' She got out this box with a lid on it that said, 'Nanny's Keepsakes,' and it was even in Nanny's handwriting. I asked where this had been, and Mother said it had been in the attic.

"'I remembered it after she died,' she said. 'Nanny knew she was getting close to death. I've not looked into it. Let's open it.'

"In it, I found my grandfather's ledger. He was a lawyer during the Great Depression. I looked at letters from her sons, when they had served in WWII. Precious mementos. I found her Bible, and it was marked. When I had stayed with her for a length of time, we shared the same feather mattress. I can tell you that I went to bed every night with her reading the Word of God over me.

"All these years have passed and here were her keepsakes. I pulled everything out and found about six things. There was one little white envelope at the bottom and it appeared to be empty. I picked it up, and it felt like there was nothing in it.

"'What is this?' I asked.

"My mom said, 'I have no idea, honey.'

"'Wonder if we should open it?'

"'Well, Nanny's not going to stop you! Go right ahead.'

"So I slipped my finger along the top—being so careful, because this might sound weird to you, but I could just picture my grandmother licking the envelope and sealing it.

"When I got it open, I started to say, "There's nothing in it!" But when I looked down in the corner, there was a torn piece of a picture of a little buck-toothed girl in the third grade. She had pulled that picture out of the trash, sealed it in an envelope, and put it in this box.

"I looked at my mother, as tears were streaming down my cheeks, and said, 'Why did she do that?'

"She loved all of her grandchildren. She did not love me more than the rest. We didn't have a good answer. But now I think I now know. It was hope. She did not even know all that had happened to me by that time. All she knew was that I was a troubled but sweet child in her mind. I believe she pulled out that picture and prayed over me and sealed that picture in an envelope and said, 'I will never see what You do with this child...but I can hope! I can hope!'"

What a powerful illustration of the influence of a godly grandmother! Choose your words and affirmations carefully. Grandmother, your influence may touch a future international Bible teacher. It's a God thing! As my granddaughter said, "God did it!"

Dear Father, when I heard Beth tell this story on tape, I got off my walking treadmill, got on my knees, and wept, begging You to let me have this kind of influence on my grandchildren.

Let me put each of my grandchildren in Your "Treasure Box," sealed with Your love and grace. Let me live and pray in hope for all You will make of them, with or without braces. Draw them to Your everlasting love and mercy.

Precious Father, I ask You to claim the lives of my five grandchildren for Your Kingdom. I will pray daily for them.

—Esther

♥ treasures of the heart

♥ Go through your attic or basement and find old photo albums with pictures of you and other members of the family when you were young. Especially look for pictures of you and your husband. Put these precious photos in a scrapbook or picture album. Write a detailed explanation of each picture:

• What was going on in the world at the time?

• What was happening when the picture was taken?

• Who was taking the picture?

• Where was it taken?

This album will become a precious treasure to your kids and grandkids!

● pearls of wisdom

● Measure your words to your grandchildren. They can have a lifelong impact.

● Keep a treasure box of art, letters, and notes from your grandkids. Someday they will find them and be blessed that you kept them safe!

Dee Dah Day!

In his inspiring book, *The Life You've Always Wanted*, John Ortberg tells a wonderful story. It makes this grandmother want to experience more "Dee Dah Days" in my life...and with my children and grandchildren. Read and enjoy!

~

"Some time ago I was giving a bath to our three children. I had a custom of bathing them together, more to save time than anything else. I knew that eventually I would have to stop 'group bathing,' but for the time being, it seemed efficient.

"Johnny was in the tub. Laura was out and safely in her pajamas. I was trying to get Mallory dried off. Mallory was out of the water, but was doing what has come to be known in our family as the Dee Dah Day dance. This consists of her running round and round in circles, singing over and over again, 'Dee Dah Day! Dee Dah Day!' It is a relatively simple dance, expressing her great joy. When she is too happy to hold it any longer, or when words are inadequate to give voice to her euphoria, she has to dance to release her joy. So, she does the Dee Dah Day routine.

"On this particular occasion, I was irritated. 'Mallory! Hurry!' I prodded. So she did—she began running in circles faster and faster and chanting 'Dee Dah Day' more rapidly. 'No, Mallory! That's not what I mean! Stop with the Dee Dah Day stuff, and get over here so I can dry you off. Hurry!'

"Then she asked a most profound question: 'Why?'

"I had no answer. I had nowhere to go...nothing to do...no meeting to attend and no sermon to write. I was just so used to the 'art of hurrying,' so preoccupied with my own little agenda...so trapped in this rat race of moving from one task to another, that here was life, here was joy, and here was the invitation to the dance—right in front of me—and I was missing it!

"So I got up...and Mallory and I did the Dee Dah Day dance together. She said I was pretty good at it...for a man my age!"

"My hold you, Nana."

—Walker, age two, reaching his hands up

♥ treasures of the heart

♥ Be quiet and still. Think of a way you would like to spend a "Dee Dah Day." Go to a movie, have tea with a friend, eat lunch with your sweetheart, read a book, look through a family scrapbook, clean a closet. Go ahead and do it now! Enjoy your "Dee Dah Day!"

♥ Read Emilie Barnes' book, *The Spirit of Loveliness*. It's a treasure full of pearls of wisdom, just for you. We grandmothers must nurture and take care of ourselves. This book will help.

_____

_____

_____

_____

_____

_____

_____

_____

_____

_____

_____

 treasure in a box

• Sow seeds of kindness, and they will grow to seeds of love.

• Read with a grandchild, snuggled together in a down comforter.

• Share tea with a friend.

• Visit a shut-in, and take your puppy.

You're Somebody Special Here

I was given the middle name of my mother's mother, "Esther." Grandmother Woods was my "downtown" grandmother. Her husband was a coal miner. Her home was small. I can still hear the sound of her cinder sidewalk that led to the swinging gate. I spent many hours on that gate. And I can still recall the fragrance of her "sunshine-dried" sheets.

The outhouse was not far from the house, but seemed very far to me! We had our baths in the kitchen sink. We were fortunate, as Grandmother had an "inside pump." (On my paternal grandparents' farm, the water pump was outside the back door. Our bath water had to be heated on a coal-burning stove.)

Saturday night was bath night at Grandmother Woods'. (My grandchildren cannot even imagine that. Yet at times, they might prefer just one bath a week!) Grandmother bathed me, then dressed me in fresh, clean pajamas. Then came the ritual of putting my hair in "rags," so I would have ringlets for Sabbath day. I had naturally curly hair, so the Saturday "do" would last me all week!

Sunday morning after breakfast, my grand-mother would dress me and then cover my dress with a little white lace apron. Then she brushed my hair, making ringlets around her fingers, and finishing off with a bow. I thought quite highly of myself, and I cherished this weekly ritual.

I happen to be a twin. My twin brother, David, was born 6 1/2 hours before me. That's right—6 1/2 hours! I was born in the "dark ages," when there was no such thing as a sonogram. I don't know who was more surprised—my mother, my father, or the doctor when, 6 1/2 hours after giving birth to my brother, my mother went back into labor. They had not realized I was in there! (I am so glad they found me!)

My brother and I were born on February 6. Our older sister turned one year old on February 20. And that is not all! The next March, our baby brother, Bob, was born. My precious moth-er had four children in less than three years. Then, fourteen years later, my mother went to the hospital, thinking she had appendicitis. But a few months later she delivered a baby sister to this now-teenaged group of older siblings. (I was not happy about this. I said, "You can't have a baby! You are a *mother*!!!") At fourteen, I was embarrassed.

～

But back to my original story...

My brother was not strong at birth, having had some breathing trouble. Grandmother Esther came and cared for us, and many times I went home with her. It was after one such long visit with her that I learned some lessons about being part of a large family. I fully expected my mother to curl my hair around her fingers and place a bow in my hair, just as Grandmother Esther had done. When she didn't do this, I protested: "Grandmother puts a bow in my hair every morning!"

"Well," Mother responded, as she hastily brushed my hair, "you're nobody special here! You're just one of the bunch."

I was devastated! I thought about running away from home, but did not know how to get to my grandmother's house! The truth was, I was just one of the bunch. With four of us in cloth diapers, no day care, and no nursery, Mother was doing the best she could.

Now I thank God for my mother. I often ask my father how she did it. One of my favorite memories were the special birthday cakes. Mother would hide little metal toys (they were metal back then!) wrapped in wax paper in the birthday cake. And the birthday child always got a nickel! I was mesmerized by how Mother always knew where the nickel was. That was a huge treat back then. A nickel would buy an ice cream cone!

I learned that my mother's spiritual gift was faith. She often said, "We'll just turn that over to God." As a child, I knew that whenever my mother prayed, God would answer because He knew her personally. She always gave Him the glory.

Looking back now, I believe I received much of my sense of well-being from my grandmother Mildred Esther Woods. While in her home, I got special attention. I loved going to her house. Whenever I arrived, I'd run to her from the car and she would sweep me into her bosom and hold me tightly. I can still remember her fragrance. She poured her love into my life, reading to me and praying with me. She dressed me up daily and allowed me to cook with her. She had a sewing room on the screened-in back porch. I can still see her on her knees by the daybed in that sewing room.

~

Grandmothers, perhaps, are a little like God:

They rejoice in the creation of a grandchild.
They accept their grandchildren as a gift from God.
They love unconditionally.
They take plenty of time with their grandchildren.
Once in a while they do the "Dee Dah Day" dance!

God can't be everywhere,
so He made grandmothers.

It is a great gift when grandparents are connected to their grandchildren. Our grandchildren have made a big difference in our lives. I want to pass on cherished memories for my grandchildren! How about you?

"My grandmother, whom we lovingly called Mamaw, used to say to me when I was being helpful, 'Why, you're as handy as a pocket in a shirt!' She lived to be 97 years old. I loved Mamaw's saying because I knew the value of a pocket for holding treasures, and it made me feel valued."

—*Patsy Clairmont, author*

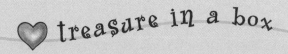
treasure in a box

The Other Cheek

On hearing indignant wails from the kitchen, I looked in to see what was happening. Bunny, age three, was holding her hand to her cheek and eyeing Anne reproachfully.

"What on earth's the matter?" I demanded.

"Mommy," replied five-year-old Anne patiently. "I'm teaching Bunny about the Bible. I'm slapping her on one cheek and teaching her to turn the other one so I can slap it, too."

—*Ruth Bell Graham,*
It's My Turn

Grandfather's Bible

My father served in the ministry as a pastor for 40-plus years. He and my mother were married almost 62 years before mother died from Alzheimer's disease in 1996. My mother partnered with my father all those years in the ministry, and for many years after retirement accompanied him on short-term missions trips.

Mother asked me one day before her death if I ever speak to groups of ministers' wives. I replied that occasionally I have that opportunity. Thinking to herself for a moment, she then said, "This younger generation is different, isn't it?" I agreed.

Mother was in her eighties at this time. She went on to tell me that she had spoken to a group of young ministers' wives, and had told them that every Sabbath morning she would lay out my father's clothes on the bed for him—his suit, tie, handkerchief, shoes, and socks. She was taken aback when the women began laughing, saying, "Let him dress himself!" Quietly she said to me, "I never did tell them why I did that."

"It is a different day and time, Mother," I responded. "But I've always wanted to know why you did that, too. I thought it was in the minister's handbook, on page seven!"

She then shared with me what I perceive to be the secret of their long ministry together: "I laid out your father's clothes so he would have more time on his knees before he opened the Word of God to the people of God."

...Whew!

I wonder what might happen if we mothers and wives would always make special preparation for our families on Sundays, to help prepare them to hear the Word of God, or to help prepare our pastor-husbands to deliver the Word of God?

And what might happen if, on Monday mornings, our husbands were to fix the lunches so that we wives and mothers could spend a little more time on our knees for our children as they go out into the world?

My father—now 96—still meets his heavenly Father on his knees every morning. In fact, on a recent visit I walked by his study room and there he was—studying the Word as if he had to preach on Sunday. He loves God's Word!

I have always been intrigued with my father's study notations throughout his Bible. His old Bible is fragile from much use. One day I said, "Daddy, I would like to have your Bible after you are gone, to give it to your namesake grandson, David Lloyd."

My father cleared his throat and answered, "Your twin brother has already asked for my Bible."

Rightly so, I thought. *My twin, David, is Daddy's oldest son and a good Bible teacher himself. He should have Dad's Bible.* But I was a little disappointed.

In 1998, my Father—at 91—remarried! His bride, Eunice, had been a close friend to my parents. In fact, at one time my father had been her interim pastor. All five of my brothers and sisters were at the wedding, along with their children and grandchildren. At the wedding ceremony, we stood as witnesses for Daddy. And Eunice's grandchildren and great-grandchildren stood as her witnesses.

You would have loved this picture: the entire front of the church was literally filled with family. I've never been to a wedding where, when the minister pronounced them "man and wife," an instant standing ovation resulted!

Our son David is an ordained minister and was asked by his granddad to be a part of the wedding ceremony. When my son walked out in his black robe and beautiful handmade stole from Africa to stand with his grandfather, my eyes filled with tears. Here was my son, participating in the marriage ceremony for his grandfather!

David told the congregation what he knew about his grandfather. Then he began to share how he had come to know Eunice through her book.

Eunice had served in Africa—where David's wife, Colleen, had grown up. Eunice is well known for her hospitality. She loved cooking for the missionaries. As David began to share about Eunice cooking lots of good food for the missionaries, he proceeded to get all choked up. He handed his notes to the pastor, saying, "This is good stuff! You read it!" As the pastor began reading what David had written, he also became teary—so David took it back and finished it.

"Granddad," David said, "when you married Colleen and me, you gave us three words: leave, cleave, and weave. Now I give these words back to you and Miss Eunice. I have seen the nationals in Africa weaving baskets. When they weave three strands together, the basket becomes stronger."

Beautiful words from a grandson to his grandfather. There was not a dry eye in the place.

～

Little did David know at the time that his grandfather had bought a new Bible and had been copying every word from his old Bible to give to David. It took him five years to finish the project! What a treasure my son was given by his grandfather. I call it "passing on a heritage of faith to the next generation." It is a grandparent thing, dear reader!

I have a wonderful photo of my father holding Walker Lloyd Burroughs, my son David's son, and reading to him from a children's Bible. When Walker and Milligan were little babies, David asked their great grandfather to pray a blessing over them. Colleen captured his words on tape. This blessing was an intimate moment—a pearl of great price.

♥ treasures of the heart

♥ Have you thought about a grandchild to whom you might give your Bible? Have you used a devotional book through the years that might have your tearstains and notes, such as *Streams in the Desert*, or *My Utmost for His Highest*? Do you have a grandchild who would cherish one of these treasures? Consider inscribing on the front cover the name of the grandchild to whom you wish to give it. Include the date of your inscription, and perhaps add a little love note.

_____

_____

_____

_____

_____

The Touch of a Voice

David and Colleen were going off on a ski trip. This would be the very first time they had left the twins since their birth two-and-one-half years earlier. They really needed time away—together. I could feel Colleen's anxiety as she pieced together the childcare for the twins. A mother's heart is never quite settled when she leaves her children, especially for the first time.

I promised to pray hourly for their protection and care—they were constantly on my mind. While reading a *Woman's Day* magazine on an airplane, I happened to notice an article entitled "Tips for Grandparents"—suggestions for how to stay in touch with grandkids. The article suggested simply reading them stories on audiotape!

That was it! I decided right then that when I got back home, while their parents were still away, I would send the twins "Nana's voice" by reading them a book on tape.

I went to the local bookstore and purchased two age-appropriate books. My husband's assignment was to borrow a tape recorder so I could make this happen! I was in a hurry. I wanted this to arrive the second day the parents were away, and I knew how they loved reading books.

When we got back home and were ready to tape, I practiced a little. Then Bob set everything up for me. (It's amazing what a grandfather will do for his grandkids!) After completing both tapes, I labeled them with the book titles, signed them "by Nana," and sent them by overnight delivery. (As my daughter-in-law says, "Only a grandmother would do that!") My task complete, I set about preparing for my next speaking engagement in South Florida.

Later that week, while in Florida, I noticed that my phone had a message. Turning it on, I heard Colleen's voice—full of tears. "I can't believe you did that. Thank you for sending my children your voice on tape while I was gone, so they would hear a familiar voice! What a treasure you have given me...and them. Now they will have this tape for their children to hear their great-grandmother's voice some day!"

I had never thought of that possibility. A double blessing!

Colleen's message bought back to me another "voice message" memory. When the twins were three months old, Colleen took a day-trip out of town. David was to be "Mr. Mom" that day. (I love how this young generation parents together.) David had asked us to pray for him and the twins. It would be their first experience to nurse from a bottle.

I prayed and then, of course, called a little after the ten o'clock feeding. David shared that Milligan had taken the bottle with no problem—but Walker would have nothing to do with it. "But Mom," he hurried on, "Colleen called at 10:00 P.M. and I told her the problem. She told me to put the phone to his ear. Then she began to talk to Walker. When she did, he began to take the bottle!"

The awesome power of a mother's voice!

How much this is like our Heavenly Father. He desires to comfort us as a mother comforts a child of her womb. How often the sound of His voice from the Word has comforted and nourished this grandmother. His voice is clear to me and my heart thirsts to hear His every Word. I often feel like the psalmist: *"My soul thirsts for Thee, my flesh longs for Thee in a dry and weary land"* (Psalm 63:1).

~

Imagine a God who cares for us as a mother cares for her child! What more could we ask? Listen to God's words for the children of Israel: *"For this is what the LORD says, 'I will extend peace to her like a river, and the wealth of nations like a flooding stream; you will nurse and be carried on her arm and dandled on her knees. As a mother comforts her child, so will I comfort you; and you will be comforted over Jerusalem' "* (Isaiah 66:12–13 NIV).

♥ treasures of the heart

♥ Borrow some of your grandchildren's favorite books or purchase a couple of age-appropriate books. Record your voice as you read these books to them. Yes, it does take time and energy, but what a treasure it will be to your grandchildren!

♥ Record yourself reading a chapter book for an older grandchild. What a gift for a grandchild—to hear a grandparent's voice reading a whole chapter of a favorite book! Of course, let the granddad read some chapters, too!

♥ If you are into videotaping, make a video recording of yourself reading the book.

_____

_____

_____

_____

_____

_____

_____

_____

_____

_____

Tea for Two...or Four... or Six (Not Counting Dolls and Bears)

Growing up in Canada, I enjoyed "tea time" as a daily ritual. I love visiting England, and having "high tea" in the late afternoon. It's a virtual display of dainty goodies, all enticing and so delicious. It can be simple as a biscuit or very lavish, with petit fours and sandwiches. No wonder the British eat supper late in the evening!

One of the treasures I inherited from my mother is a teacup with bright yellow daffodils. It is my custom, on a winter afternoon and anytime I'm writing, to stop for afternoon tea and drink from my mother's cup. I like the connection.

Planning our second year of Nana's Summer Camp, I just had to include in the schedule an afternoon tea party. Aunt Colleen also has a tea tradition, having grown up in Africa, and she has wonderful tea stories to share. She agreed to help.

Throughout the year, I was on the lookout for tea-party things. I found a teapot, place cards, and little place card holders with tiny spoons with teapot handles. So precious these were! When the day for the tea party arrived, the older girls made tiny name cards. I set the table with a linen tablecloth and gathered flowers from the garden for a centerpiece.

For another year's tea party, I sent an invitation to each grandchild's American Girl doll or special teddy bear. The invitation stated "Party dresses, please." I bought doll hats as a surprise, so the dolls would be "properly dressed" for the tea party. That year, we set a table for the grandchildren and a table for the dolls and bears, with their own name place cards and tiny china tea sets! Each grandchild was responsible to host her doll, as well as to be a guest herself.

What treasured times these were! For just a few minutes, we were transported to our pretend world, joining our hearts with grandmothers of other centuries who shared tea time and stories with their grandchildren.

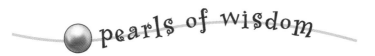

pearls of wisdom

Remember: most of the fun in having a tea party is in the preparation and then in spending unhurried time together.

♥ treasures of the heart

♥ Have a special tea-party time together with your grandchildren, and take photos of this from beginning to end. Make up "British lady names" and speak with a British accent. Make tea parties a regular event with your grandchildren. Write down your memories of these days.

_____

_____

_____

_____

_____

_____

_____

_____

_____

_____

_____

_____

_____

_____

_____

_____

_____

Tears from a Grandfather's Heart

"For whoever wants to save his life will lose it, but whoever loses his life for me will save it."

~

—Luke 9:24 NIV

It was Bob's idea: We would give our granddaughters and their parents a "Disney World Christmas." We happened to have a very close friend who worked at the Magic Kingdom. We made the call, confirmed our reservations, and sent a letter of invitation to our daughter's family. Everyone was excited about this early Christmas gift!

We chose to go the week following Thanksgiving. "Wilderness Lodge" was to be our home for three days and four nights.

Our first idea had been to take just the two oldest girls, who at the time were $5^1/2$ and $7^1/2$ —perfect Disney ages! At the last minute, however, we decided to include Frances, who was only 3^1/$_2$. What a gift that decision turned out to be! We got to see the Magic Kingdom through the eyes of a little girl who still believed in the Disney Magic—and I mean *really believed*!

We also got to be the "Grand Marshals" for one of the afternoon Disney parades. This meant we got to ride in an open-air car at the front of the parade. The two big girls laughed at younger Frances, who chose to wear her brand new "101 Dalmatians" pajamas as her outfit that day! The crowd loved it.

We met a wonderful man, Ray, who was the parade master. Ray is a cancer survivor, a Christian, and has an enormous joy in life. We were also privileged to share the Grand Marshall honors with a family from New Jersey and their precious special-needs daughter named Fulani.

Fulani was very tiny and had a tiny little voice. It made you want to hold her so you wouldn't miss a word she said. Such joy filled her face as we made the trip down Main Street. Her entire family was invited to be guests of Disney and the "Make-a-Wish Home." We learned that each night at the Make-a-Wish Home, Disney characters come to read bedtime stories to the children and have a prayer time with them.

At the end of the parade we were taken to a holding area to wait for all the parade characters. Everyone was told that they could dance with any character they chose as the characters stepped off their floats.

The wait was excruciating for the little ones! Fulani sat on the curb—her feet barely touching the pavement—under the watch care of her teenage brother...a tender sight. While we waited, our girls went over to speak to Fulani and her family. She told them that she was having her best day ever!

As the parade came to an end, the characters stepped off the float and the children rushed forward to choose a dance partner. Then I saw Prince Charming step off his float and head straight to the sidewalk where Fulani was sitting. He picked her up and danced her all over the road, as everyone cheered. I could hardly photograph my grandchildren, as tears spilled from my eyes. When the music ended, the prince kissed Fulani and placed her in her father's arms.

The parade was not about us. It was about sharing a treasured moment with a special little angel named Fulani. My girls knew the significance of that day.

Later that evening, Bob and I took the girls to a special Disney Christmas Dinner Theater with cast and characters. It was pure delight. We were one table of many grandparents with grandchildren—out for an evening of memories. Santa showed up and gave away gifts, and we sang Christmas carols. It was an enchanted evening, to be sure.

But the real gift of the evening happened when little Frances, who was sitting in her granddad's lap, leaned over and whispered, "I love you, Bop. I love you." I watched as tears softly fell down Bob's cheeks, and thought, *What if we had left her home...thinking she was too little!*

~

This may sound like just a Nana story, but it is also a God story. God tells us over and over, "I love you, Child. I love you." God's journey to the cross through His Son tells us of His eternal love—a treasure that can never be taken away from us.

note from Frances, age 6

 treasures of the heart

♥ Make a memory for a special-needs child in your church or neighborhood. Plan a day to take the child and his or her mother to a Christmas show, to the zoo, or to a movie. If you can also take your grandchildren, all will be blessed.

♥ Check to see if you can spend an afternoon helping at a homeless shelter or tutoring a child. Make a difference in the life of some child who might need a "Nana."

_____

_____

_____

_____

_____

_____

_____

_____

_____

_____

_____

_____

_____

_____

Time Out

*"All discipline for the moment seems
not to be joyful, but sorrowful; yet
to those who have been trained by it,
afterwards, it yields the peaceful
fruit of righteousness."*

~

—*Hebrews 12:11* NASB

My generation was not told about "time out." We just knew the "switch" or the belt. Then we were sent to the corner—to ponder the error of our ways, I suppose. It worked!

I first learned about "time out" as each of my granddaughters was born. I am relearning it again with the grandtwins.

To observe my grandtwins has been a fun journey for me, as I am a twin myself. In their very early months of life, I was privileged to spend a few weeks with David and Colleen to help. At the 5:30am feedings, I would listen at the foot of the steps as they nursed. When I heard their mother's soft voice talking, I knew Milligan was finished. I would slip up, take her

note from Milligan and Walker, age 3

downstairs, burp her, diaper her, and get her settled in the downstairs crib. Then I would repeat the same process with Walker, so Colleen could rest.

The twins slept in the same crib. I was fascinated by them, and would stand over their crib just marveling. Their hands were always in the same position. When one turned his or her head, so would the other. They seemed to shadow each other's movements!

Bob wanted to write a song for their baby dedication, and asked me to write the lyrics. I said, "Just let me get there and see them, and I will get inspired." And I did. The words came to me early one morning...

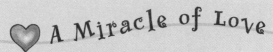

A Miracle of Love

by Esther Burroughs

Intimately given from the heart of God,
Knit together in the parents' love.
Tiny hands, tiny feet,
Such a miracle of love.

Perfectly formed by the hand of God,
How precious are His works of grace.
Little smiles, breath so sweet,
Such a miracle of love.

Skillfully kept by the love of God
As we journey on His path of love.
Guided by His truth and grace,
Such a miracle of love.

May our families give you praise
For your awesome, fearful ways.
May our families give you praise
Guided by your holy ways.

As they grew, the twins developed a language only they understood. I'd listen early in the mornings as they chatted back and forth. I know they understood each other because they answered each other. Milligan would tilt her head as she spoke to Walker. He always answered. It must have been a special "twins language."

I am now seeing them take care of each other.

"It be yor twurn, Walker."

"Now it my twurn, Millie."

Milligan is often in charge. Oh yes, and they also hit each other.

When they were two, if Walker was put in time out—and he most often was the one in time out—Milligan would pull up a chair and sit beside him. Is that cute or what? Walker has a tender heart and his words can melt you down. This is not true with Milligan! She can stare you down—not melt you down—with the best of them. Recently, Walker hit Milligan—and then put himself in time out! Now that's a new one for me!

After a good laugh, I reflected on the fact that God, the Father, sits with us in "time out," too. Surely He must tire of my consistent disobedience, as He hears the immature child in me say, "I do it myself!"

But even though He disciplines us for our own good, God took our place on the cross—so that we would never have to go there. What love! He gave the gift of His Holy Spirit—to empower us to live a mature disciplined life, so we can become like Him. What comfort! He has prepared a home for us in His presence, and in the meantime longs to see our faces, just for fellowship! What devotion!

Ask God today to help you walk in holiness. Dwell on His Word, dear grandmother. It will arm you with strength and endurance to finish the race.

_____

_____

_____

_____

_____

_____

_____

"I know God will not give me anything I can't handle. I just wish that he didn't trust me so much."

~

—*Mother Teresa*

♥ treasures of the heart

♥ When appropriate, share with a grandchild about a time when their parent was disciplined. Laugh and learn together. It will encourage your grandchild, helping them know that parents are people, too. You might even tell them a story about yourself.

_____

_____

_____

_____

_____

_____

_____

_____

_____

_____

_____

_____

_____

_____

_____

_____

_____

26

Honoring a Great Aunt—
A Grandmother to Many

We had gathered to honor my Aunt Mary, whom we call "Birdie." She is a single woman who once worked as a business school professor. Birdie is my father's only sister. In January of 2001, she turned 98. Every niece and nephew has a needlepoint picture in his or her home that Birdie has made. Some have crocheted tablecloths.

Birdie is the one who paid for her grand-nieces and nephews to have piano lessons. I know—I had them and hated them! When we gathered at the farm, the last thing in the evenings—right before Bible reading and prayers—Aunt Birdie would always insist that each of the children play the piano or whatever instrument they were learning. Of course we should play for her—she was paying for our music lessons!

As children, we did not know that Birdie was teaching us to stand up and perform and share our gifts. Now I am most grateful. She corrected the grammar in our letters to her, sending them back so we could learn. She is the proud auntie of nine nieces and nephews—and some thirty grandnieces and nephews. Her role has been much like a grandmother.

As my family gathered to celebrate her birthday, everyone was invited to share a memory from his or her life about Auntie. It was a teary and tender evening. She would say, "Oh stop it!" But her tears and laughter bespoke her enjoyment.

Then my cousin Ian stood to speak. His wife read his story, because he could never have made it through his tears. Of all the cousins, this man has a most tender heart. He has worked at keeping our family connected, though it was Auntie's idea to start these reunions some twenty years ago. Ian invited Auntie Mary to come and stand beside him. She fussed a bit but stood up and came. Then he put his arm around her shoulder and handed her a glass of water, saying, "I want to toast you." They lifted their glasses high as he said, "To Aunt Birdie!"—to our enthusiastic applause.

Then Ian looked at Birdie and said, "A few years ago, you and I were talking about the old home place—and you mentioned how much you would like just one more drink from the spring on the old homestead." She nodded, remembering. He said, "Well, you've just had one!" A hush fell over the family.

This nephew had truly honored his Aunt. He had made a long trip to the homestead, knocked on the door of the present owners, and asked permission to gather a bucket of water from the old spring. Silently we looked on as he uncovered the bucket of water from the old spring, which had been carried many miles to honor this Auntie, who had all her life honored God through her life of service.

~

I was reminded of King David doing battle with the Philistines. As he hid in a cave of Adullam he said, "Oh, that someone would give me water to drink from the well of Bethlehem, which is by the gate." The story then tells of three mighty men, breaking through the enemy line, drawing water from that well and bringing it back to their king. When they presented it to him, David would not drink, but instead poured it out on the ground to the Lord. David was overwhelmed by the faithfulness of his men— who had put their lives at risk for him (2 Samuel 23:13–17).

Most of the time I'm like David—longing for a drink from the wells at Bethlehem. Think about it: I can open God's Word daily, drink from the riches of His grace, and be completely satisfied. Some days may be like breaking through the enemy line, but the risk is worth the reward of being satisfied by the Living Water. I think of the words of Isaiah 58:11: "*And the* Lord *will continually guide you, And satisfy your desire in scorched places, And give strength to your bones; And you will be like a watered garden, And like a spring of water whose waters do not fail."*

Later that evening, as the cousins laughed and shared about the stories we had told about Auntie, something dawned on all of us: Each one of us thought we were Auntie's favorite! What a rare gift—to make all your grandnieces, grandnephews, and grandchildren feel as if he or she is your favorite.

Anna: "I wish Nana was my mother."

Anna's Mother: "No, you don't!
When she was my mother,
she was mean!"

♥ treasures of the heart

♥ Think of a way to serve your mate, a friend, or a grandchild today—just for the joy of serving and blessing another.

_____

_____

_____

_____

_____

_____

_____

_____

_____

_____

_____

_____

● pearls of wisdom

● *"For even the Son of Man did not come to be served, but to serve, and to give His life a ransom for many."* —Mark 10:45 NIV

27

Feed the Soil, and the Soil Will Feed You in Return

Leonard Sweet, in his book *A Cup of Coffee at the Soul Café*, talks about Sunday traditions at the home of his grandparents. His grandmother's way of putting the need to "hallow" some time in our lives was by announcing, "Now's Sabbath time." Life needs fallow fields, green spaces, and empty places. We all need a break from the business of making an effort. Sweet says, "Feed the soil, and the soil will feed you in return. Feed the soul, and the soul will feed you in return."

Gramma liked to work hard. When people said to her, "You work so hard!" she would say in return, "I'm going to take my vacation in heaven." But Gramma also knew the principle of Sabbath time. Brought up in a Baptist home, Gramma was rigid about her Lord's Day. My aunts, uncles, and we grandkids couldn't even file a fingernail on Sunday! There was no ball playing, no hide-and-seek, no running wild through the house. We had to stay dressed up in our Sunday best—all day.

A Sunday schedule at Gramma's went something like this. It began like every other day, with a tradition of early rising. At 7:00 AM the family would gather around the big table, everyone dressed in his or her best clothes. Whenever the Boggs clan gathered together, Granddad would ask the Lord's blessing. Gramma could read the Scriptures, but she never prayed at the table. At the sound of "Amen," everyone would dive into a feast of bacon, eggs, biscuits, oatmeal, or on special days, mush or hominy grits—a breakfast treat Gramma cooked on the giant wood stove that she loved.

No one got up from the table until Granddad had led everyone in family prayer. Then the chairs would be pushed back and everyone would kneel at the table for a time of Bible reading and more prayer. While the table was cleared, the rest of us would put on the finishing touches for church.

Sunday afternoon was the primary time for visiting relatives and friends in neighboring "hollers," playing the pump organ and singing hymns around the piano. On special occasions Gramma would get out her dulcimer or banjo. Even more special were the times she and Granddad would sing duets! There was also a Boggs family tradition—helping out small country churches by leading worship and singing at 3:00 P.M. services.

When I was growing up, I protested the strictness of these Sunday regulations. Today, they are some of my most pleasant memories. We all need to set aside desert days—fallow fields that are not being constantly plowed up by our agendas and ambitions. Recreation means re-creation—supplying your whole body with the energy you need to be creative. Recreation literally "re-creates your soul."

~

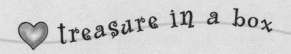

While in a seminary church situation, Bob was to be gone over a Sunday. When he told a friend he'd be away, the friend's small daughter tugged on Bob's coat, looked up and said, "But Mr. Bob, who will preach the songs?"

~

Leonard Sweet's story takes my heart and mind back to my growing-up home. We had the same respect for the Sabbath. It was the "Lord's day," my mother always said. Some things about Sabbath day at our home always stayed the same:

1. We prepared for Sabbath on Saturday.
2. The table was set with linen and the best dishes.
3. Everyone took a nap.
4. One of the four of us always got a spanking.

~

I was an adult before I realized that a spanking was not on the order of worship of a Baptist church! Every few weeks, we all traveled up to the country schoolhouse church, where Dad would preach. And we would never leave someone's home until Dad read the Word of God and prayed with the family that had hosted us.

I have many warm memories of eating with friends, in our home and in theirs. What great fun it was! We often ended by singing around the piano. Sundays were often long days, but our hearts were full and satisfied.

♥ treasures of the heart

♥ Invite your family, and if possible, your pastor's family for Sunday dinner—the old-fashioned kind! Use your best china and linen. Make a memory. Perhaps include the single mother or father with children. End with a worship service of singing, Scripture reading, and a prayer or two—with a testimony to God's goodness thrown in!

⬤ pearls of wisdom

⬤ Ask God to show you a way to have a time of worship the next time you have company. Simply reading the Bible after dinner and blessing your company and/or family in prayer might be sufficient. You'll be "feeding the soul."

⬤ Bless your family or friends with pearls of wisdom expressed specifically for them. Do not leave words unsaid that your soul feels you must express as a gift for life. These will indeed be treasures of the heart.

A Family Christmas Retreat

In the mid-seventies, while returning from a volunteer pastoring position in an English-speaking church in the Bahamas, my parents came to spend Christmas in our home in Birmingham, Alabama. During our years in music ministry, my husband served in a local church, while at the same time my father was pastoring churches before and after his retirement. This meant, of course, that our families spent very few Christmas holidays together. My children had not grown up living close to either set of their grandparents.

Working with college students at the time, I had learned how to plan retreats for students. As Christmas approached, I got to thinking: Why not do plan a *family* Christmas retreat, right here in our home?

Together, Bob and I planned the family retreat in great detail. David was nine years old at the time; Melody was thirteen. My goal was to help my children get to know their grandparents more intimately.

The first night of the retreat was "game night." Fun and laughter reigned. Each of us named our favorite childhood games. What fun it was to discover games that were played in the early 1900s—on the farm and with no electricity. Then each person had to tell about the most exciting Christmas he or she had experienced.

In preparation for the second night, we baked goodies to be delivered to our neighbors that evening. The grandparents helped wrap the special packages of cookies and cake for our neighbors. After supper, off we went! The Christmas lights in the neighborhood made our journey both easier and festive.

I had given the neighbors a "heads up" that we were coming before their children's bedtime. We started at the top of the street. Our young Jewish neighbors welcomed us joyfully, and we had enclosed a Hanukkah card in their package. We sang "Jingle Bells" and "White Christmas," accompanied by Bob on his ukulele! Tabitha, our cat, followed us to each house. We sang to Methodists, Baptists, a Lutheran, some Catholics, and to some families who did not attend church. Christmas carols cross all denominational lines! It was a fun evening.

The next morning, some neighbors who loved the singing Von Trapp family of *The Sound of Music* called and said, "You have started a tradition as the 'Von Burroughs Family' and you must come next year." We did.

The third evening, we talked about the

Christmas traditions we'd grown up with. Our children not only learned about my childhood home, but also about the families my parents grew up with. It was a treasured time indeed.

The last evening of the retreat was Christmas Eve. Bob had built a cozy fire in the fireplace, and eggnog and goodies were on hand. I divided us into three teams—two persons on each team. My father and our son David were to look up Luke 2 and pretend that David was the young son of the innkeeper. He was to stand behind the door as Mary and Joseph asked for a room. They were to tell the story through the eyes of a nine-year-old boy.

The next assignment went to Melody and my mother. Melody was to pretend she was the fourteen-year-old Mary, and that she had to explain—to her mother!—about the angel's visit and that she was to be the Christ child's mother.

Bob and I were to rewrite the Luke 2 account as if it appeared in our morning newspaper that year—1978. We discovered a wonderful way to experience Christmas through new eyes, bringing the story into our hearts in a new and fresh way. In the process, our children gleaned insight and traditions from their grandparents that they might not otherwise have had. It was a treasured Christmas retreat.

♥ treasures of the heart

♥ Plan a retreat like this with your children and grandchildren—sharing your generation's Christmas stories and traditions. Make up your own schedule. Be as creative as you like. All it takes is a bit of time and preparation.

♥ Share a childhood photo book of some of your childhood Christmases, and compare customs and traditions. This might begin a new tradition.

⬤ pearls of wisdom

⬤ Read Charles Dickens' *A Christmas Carol* to your grandkids.

⬤ Attend a performance of *A Christmas Carol* resented by a dinner theater or church drama group in your community. It truly teaches the Christmas spirit!

_____

_____

_____

Be Ye Kind, 1, 2, 3

I remember teaching this Bible verse to my granddaughter, Frances: *"Be ye kind one to another"* (Ephesians 4:32 KJV). Frances is bright, and learns quickly. Wanting to show her off to her dad as he came in the door, I said, "Frances, say your Bible verse for Daddy."

Softly, she began, "Be kind, one...um. Be kind one, um. ...Be kind, one, two, three, four!" lifting her hands in joy. A child's treasure—and a godly truth.

Paul wrote to the Colossians, *"Clothe yourselves with compassion, kindness, humility, gentleness, and patience. Bear with each other and forgive whatever grievances you may have against one another."* (3:12–13 NIV)

"Always be a little kinder than necessary." I found this quote somewhere, and immediately cut it out to put on my desk. (I need constant reminders!) That led me to make a poster for the fridge, my bathroom mirror, and the dashboard of my car: "Kindness rules!"

It is often difficult to act in kindness. But God desires that we be kind—one, two, three times, and a whole lot more. What might happen if the "kinder than necessary" rule applied in our homes, at school, at play, and at work?

Father, empower us to act as ones
appointed by You—with a heart
of kindness and gentleness,
bearing with one another.

~

Read Colossians 3:12–14 from THE MESSAGE translation. Wow!

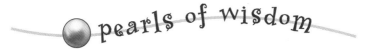

pearls of wisdom

Children learn by imitation. Pass on the gift of kindness.

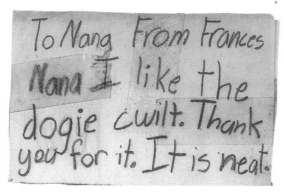

To Nana From Frances
Nana I like the
dogie cwilt. Thank
you for it. It is neat.

note from Frances, age 8

Just an Ice Cream Cone

The fall of 1960, Bob and I were living in Dennison, Texas. Bob was enrolled at Southwestern Baptist Theological Seminary, in the School of Church Music. He also served part-time (if there is such a thing) at Calvary Baptist Church. I was teaching and expecting our first child. It was a difficult time, made more difficult when our almost-eight-month-old baby boy was stillborn. That day was void of sunshine.

When my mother came to stay with me during the recovery time, light began to slowly return to my life. It was during this time that my mother and I became "adult friends." As we shared family stories, I felt safe to have my mother taking care of me. It's amazing how often, in tragedy, our hearts begin to open up and share, discovering each other's hurts. And just in the listening, healing begins.

I had had no idea my mother carried deep hurts in her own life, and that her mother—my grandmother—had listened and wisely counseled her through those times. I'd always thought that mothers and grandmothers were strong and could do anything. Surely one of the roles of a grandmother is to listen with her heart.

It was many years later, while on a speaking engagement in Asia, that I was able to listen, cry with, and support a young missionary wife through her loss of a baby. I was able to listen and weep with her because I had been taught well, having gone through the experience. I'll never forget her words: "Thanks for being my mom this week. I needed you so much."

Light came to me during my recovery from another direction as well. I could hear his whistle before I saw him cross the porch. There he would stand, covered in flour in his Pillsbury Flour Company hat and jacket, having just come from work.

James Johnson stood at the door and held out an ice cream cone—just for me. He didn't come in, and he didn't speak much. The very next day, he was there again. And the next. On the fourth day I asked, "James, how long are you going to bring me an ice cream cone?"

"Until your smile comes back," he said. Then he hugged me and walked away.

God whispered James' answer over and over in my heart. Healing started, and my smile did eventually return. Romans 12:10 has come to mean so much to me: *"Be devoted to one another in brotherly love. Honor one another above yourselves"* (NIV).

~

♥ treasures of the heart

♥ Who needs your smile today?

Who needs an ice cream cone?

Who needs a listening heart?

You can smile, listen, and give. Ask God to show you a young mother who needs you. Get busy grinning and sharing an ice cream. Hurt is just a phone call away. Yes, you can even smile through a phone line.

*"If I could do life over,
I would have taken more time to
listen to my grandfather ramble
about his youth."*

—*Erma Bombeck*

Family Traditions

The Burroughs Family has established many family traditions—both seasonal and non-seasonal. For instance, the Friday after Thanksgiving Day, we usually put up our Christmas tree. We string popcorn for the tree, and while the children and I decorate, Bob makes homemade ice cream, hamburgers, and fries. It's a tradition!

For a number of years we shared in a special Burroughs Family tradition. One Christmas, when our children were in their junior high years, Bob surprised us. I can't remember what year it was, but on Christmas day after all the gifts had been opened, Bob got up and began looking in the tree branches, as if searching for something. After a few moments, he brought out three small, rolled-up scrolls, each bound by a bright red ribbon and bearing one of our names. He presented a scroll to each of us. Soon we could hear sniffing sounds—as each of us read a love letter from our husband and daddy, telling us in detail how much he loved us. What a treasure this was! We continue this tradition even today, and it now includes our grandchildren when we are with them for Christmas.

I once heard about a grandmother who wrote a Christmas letter to each of her grandchildren every year—enclosing a photo of the child. I began to practice this tradition with our grandchildren. Now, as the year goes along, I make notes of things that happen to each of the grandchildren—like keeping a history of their lives. This helps me write the letter in December. I choose an appropriate card for each child, and then write a "love letter" to God, thanking Him for each grandchild and his or her special gifts. It is my way of affirming each child in his or her accomplishments during the past year. I also attach a recent photo of the child, and give them a Scripture verse, telling them that I pray this verse over them often

This is great fun—and also serves as a record of their physical growth, as well as their emotional and spiritual growth, through the year. These can also be a wonderful addition for their "life scrapbooks."

This is one way I let my grandchildren know of my love and concern as they become capable and worthy individuals in the kingdom of God. It is also a way for me to share my love for them.

_____

_____

_____

_____

_____

_____

♥ treasures of the heart

♥ Begin a Christmas or birthday letter tradition with one or more of your grandchildren. Remember: it is never too late to begin this kind of affirmation.

♥ Think of creative and innovative ways you can relate to your grandchildren, as special holidays or their birthdays approach. There are many ways a grandmother can become someone very special in the life of a grandchild!

_____

_____

_____

_____

_____

_____

_____

_____

_____

_____

_____

_____

_____

_____

_____

pearls of wisdom

A great treasure for your grandchildren is letter exchanges. Keep writing—even if they don't answer. Handwritten letters have great value! They can be read over and over. And they *will* be, I assure you!

Sept 10ᵗʰ 1934,

Dear daughter
Neva

How the world will glow
with beauty,
When love shines in
And the heart rejoice in duty
When love shines in.
Trials will be sanctified
And the soul in peace abide
Life will all be glorified
When loves shines in
with best love for
you, Mother.

note from Esther's grandmother to Esther's mother

"I Didn't Do the 'Win' One, Nana"

My Reid granddaughters are athletic as well as artistic. While living in Atlanta, they were all part of a neighborhood swim team. It sure keeps a mother busy!

Caroline, the middle child, was hesitant about the whole "swim" thing. It meant putting her head under water, and she was not sure about this. Caroline is not as competitive athletically as her sisters. She is, however, becoming quite a horsewoman. (I could also go on about her gentle, peacemaking spirit, but I won't bore you with my grandmotherly bragging!)

Caroline was placed on the "Tadpole" team. Once when I was passing through town and was going to spend the night with them, I got to spend some time at the pool, cheering for each of the grandgirls and yelling at Caroline as the whistle went off, "Get in the water! Get in the water!"

I knew there was to be another swim meet soon. I also knew her sisters would bring home all kinds of ribbons. After the meet, Caroline called me.

"Nana, I did it! I did it! I did the swim meet!"

"I am so proud of you, Caroline!" I responded. Then without thinking I asked, "Did you bring home a ribbon?"

"Nana," she answered slowly, "I didn't do the 'win' one! I only did the one where all you have to do is get in the water and swim to the end of the pool, and *everyone* gets a ribbon!"

I took a deep breath. Wouldn't life be easier if all that was required of us was just to get to the other end of the pool—simply doing our best, without pressure to earn ribbons? I do believe in competition, but wouldn't life be friendlier if we were encouraged to just do our best?

It was a great event for Caroline that day—to get in the water and make it all the way to the end of the pool. She had done well.

~

Paul confidently says, *"I have fought the good fight. I have finished the race. I have kept the faith"* (2 Timothy 4:7 NIV). He goes on to say that he has laid up for himself a crown of righteousness. Perhaps that is what today's grandparents need to remember. Life is not about winning a competition. Life is about finishing well in the kingdom of God!

♥ treasures of the heart

♥ Support and encourage your grandchildren by attending their athletic events, recitals, games, and activities whenever possible.

♥ Was anyone in your family tree athletic? Research this and share the information with an athletic grandchild.

_____

_____

_____

_____

_____

_____

_____

_____

_____

_____

_____

_____

_____

_____

_____

_____

_____

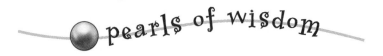

pearls of wisdom

🔘 Share stories of great athletic victories and defeats with your grandchildren and other children. They will enjoy hearing these stories from you.

🔘 Buy a bunch of multi-colored ribbons and make up your own awards for you grandkids— for no reason but love. Give such awards as "Best in Class," "Best Eater," "Best Singer," "Best Dishwasher," and "Best Hugger." They will treasure these awards from their grandmom!

🔘 Make a "Blessing Box." Fill it with simple gifts to give to anyone...at any time...for any reason.

"Do not think that love, in order to be genuine, has to be extraordinary."

～

—*Mother Teresa*

♥ tips for grandparents

1. *Compliment your grandchild in front of his or her parents—often.*

2. *Always keep your promises.*

3. *Refrain from doing two things at once. Give your grandchild your full attention.*

4. *Display proudly your grandchild's awards, trophies, art-work, and school projects.*

5. *Always give your grandchild a second (and third!) chance.*

6. *Give your child a subscription to a quality children's magazine in his or her name.*

7. *Spend a vacation with your family. Buy a travel book or video to research the destination. Let your children and grandchildren help decide what you'll see and do.*

8. *Cook with your grandchild. He or she will learn how to plan and prepare meals, and this is a great way to spend quality time together.*